CULT ESCAPE

MY JOURNEY TO FREEDOM

JOHN D SPINKS

A catalogue record for this book
Is available from the British Library
ISBN 978-1-673-69006-4

Contents

ACKNOWLEDGEMENTS

I would like to express my special thanks to the people who have helped me throughout this Cult Escape labour of love.

I spent countless hours it seems, sitting in Wetherspoons pubs, laptop plugged in, drinking coffee or ginger tea, enjoying their breakfasts and chicken, bacon, avocado salads. So, a big thank you to all the Wetherspoons chain for their comfortable 'office' that I was able to do most of my thinking and writing in.

I want to thank the most beautiful girl in the world, Heather, my daughter, for her love and encouragement. On 6th January 2019, she sent me the following text out of the blue. 'I've had this sentence going around in my head for the past few days for you: This is the year of perseverance and pushing through relentlessly.'

I was very fortunate to have been helped by someone quite brilliant, who was never a cult member, but who had an eagle-eyed perspective, always coming from the place of unconditional love. She willingly helped me shape the tone and texture of Cult Escape, including the grammatics. So many thanks to Cate Warbrick, for you I am extremely grateful.

A special thanks also to my very good friend Clive McLaren, who was always challenging my accuracy, testing my viewpoints and who helped me develop the book.

I wish to also thank all my friends who have advised me and stood by me during the writing of the book, always asking me, 'Is it finished yet?' I include the 500+ people around the world who have agreed to pray for Cult Escape. Thank you for your prayers, support and encouragement. I hope to tell you soon about the first person who has been reunited with his family after reading this book.

Also, I want to thank the 77 people who provided the quotes for the three surveys within the book. Your comments helped paint a clear picture about those issues. Thank you.

Last but not least, I want to thank my God who I used to believe was a strict, law-wielding, rules and regulations legalist , who required me to fear him, join a religion and keep separate from all who weren't up to our standard of holiness. I am thankful to have escaped from that years ago to learn that far from being religious, God is unconditional love.

Thank you!

PREFACE

Today, there are millions of precious people who are in a large variety of religious cults. Cult Escape is my personal story with a group of about 45,000 such people. The subject of cults can elicit strong feelings and I therefore want to clarify certain aspects right from the start, in an attempt to avoid misunderstandings or wrongful aspersions:

1.   Throughout the book I refer to the group I was born into as the Exclusive Brethren (EB) and not the current rebranded name since 2012; the Plymouth Brethren Christian Church (PBCC). The reason for this is that this book only covers my time and experiences within the EB which ended in November 1988. Likewise, my references to Revival Centres / Fellowships only cover my time there from December 1990 to September 1996.

2.   This book with the corresponding online resource was written from a place of love and peace towards all religious cult members, recognising the genuine sincerity in many who find themselves trapped in their situation. The fact I do not agree with everything they stand for anymore, does not mean I am attacking them personally. I am simply sharing my story, my perspectives and many of my experiences. My desire, whilst we do not see eye to eye, is that rather than take offence; we are able to dialogue openly and peacefully with the joint goal of unity.

3.   The purpose of this book is not to destroy anything or anyone. Rather it is to share my experiences, encouraging readers to make their own minds up, as to whether what goes on in some religious groups is ethical, caring and safe, or irresponsible, dangerous and abusive.

4.   This book is not telling you what to believe nor is it an academic or scientific study. To the best of my knowledge there are no exaggerations but rather the truth as I recall it from my experiences. Unconditional love affords all people their own free will to choose what they believe without judgement, even if we disagree. Therefore, I offer this book and my perspectives for your consideration and for you to make up your own mind.

DISCLAIMER

This book is a memoir and an in-depth study. It reflects the author's present recollections and some of his experiences over time. While all the stories in this book are true, some names and identifying details have been changed to protect the privacy of the people involved. The information provided in this book is designed to provide historical information and motivation to our readers on the subjects discussed. It is sold with the understanding that the author and publisher is not engaged to render any type of spiritual, psychological or any other kind of professional advice. This book is not meant to be used, nor should it be used, to diagnose or treat any mental condition. For diagnosis or treatment of any mental problem, consult your own physician. The publisher and author are not responsible for any specific spiritual or psychological health needs that may require medical supervision and are not liable for any damages or negative consequences from any treatment, action, application or preparation, to any person reading or following the information in this book. Neither the author nor the publisher shall be held liable or responsible to any person or entity with respect to any loss or incidental or consequential damages caused, or alleged to have been caused, directly or indirectly, by the information or programs contained herein. You should seek the services of a competent professional before beginning any improvement program. References are provided for informational purposes only and do not constitute endorsement of any websites or other sources. Readers should be aware that the websites listed in this book may change. Neither the publisher nor the individual author shall be liable for any physical, psychological, emotional, or commercial damages, including, but not limited to, special, incidental, consequential or other damages. Our views and rights are the same: You are responsible for your own choices, actions, and results. The author strives to present his life and experiences as truthfully as possible and references to the Exclusive Brethren, Revival Centres / Revival Fellowships, are his personal observations and beliefs and therefore his opinions and viewpoints. The book is not intended to hurt the Exclusive Brethren, Revival Centres / Revival Fellowships or any individual but rather to encourage scrutiny leading to evaluation and change, that will result in love, unity and peace like never before.

INTRODUCTION

Have you ever wondered what it must be like to be born into a strict religious cult?

My journey starts as an eight-day old baby when my mother hands me to a small swarthy man with dyed black hair. Suddenly all goes quiet and to my shock I find I cannot breathe. What is happening? I am being held under water in a full bath in my home. Now I am fully immersed into a religious cult just like my parents and grandparents were before me.

Fifty years later, I am still here to tell you the story about growing up in this 45,000-member, group that was called the Exclusive Brethren. You will get to know about my experiences of being brainwashed and my life being coercively controlled via one man, 'The Universal Leader,' also called, 'The Man of God.'

I will take you step by step through the journey of my escape at the age of 22, along with the challenges, the damaging psychological effects and the eventual healing and freedom that I am so blessed to have found. Over the years since escaping, the subject of my past has come up many times and I am used to the reaction of people which ranges from shock, disturbance, disbelief and tears. You might find it hard to believe what has been going on behind the closed doors of some of these secret groups.

In case you have not heard of the Exclusive Brethren, I start with a brief overview to give context to the story. I will show you how generally, religious cults control people's lives through indoctrination, control and evolving laws. I had to attend eleven meetings a week, 52 weeks a year. I will tell you why my school years were endured more than enjoyed. It felt like I was walking around with a tattoo on my forehead that said, 'Separation from Evil.' I recount awkward and embarrassing moments which continued into my work life. I was bound to a lifestyle of having to conform to strict rules about clothing, hair, relationships, technology, where to live, where to eat, where to sleep, what to believe and much more. Then there were the dire consequences for disobedience to any of these rules.

I have since deconstructed my escape, showing the deep psychological struggle that felt like I was a rope in a tug of war. There was no way I could lose my parents. The rope snapped when I hit the tipping point on my 22nd birthday. However, there was still the unthinkable matter of saying goodbye to my parents for maybe the last time.

Going public with this book about my past makes me feel naked and exposed. I invite you to have a look at the private parts of my life of which I am no longer ashamed. Baring all, I have discovered, brings healing and freedom that only honesty and transparency can bring. I'd recommend it to anyone.

For two years after my cult escape, I took a walk on the wild side. Now, at last I was able to explore and experiment with all the 'evils of this world' that I had been forbidden to enjoy. I even went as far as frequenting restaurants, football matches and the cinema! I had been like a tightly coiled spring that was suddenly released. Guess how long it took me to lose my virginity? How did I end up alone in London one night at a live sex show? How did I get to be taken hostage by a gang and held at knifepoint for four hours, and why did I run up a phone bill of £3500? I am here to tell you that there is life outside the cult you are in. You might have to make a few mistakes along the way, though you can learn from a few of mine if you like.

I invite you to explore questions such as; what really is a cult? What is the blind spot that causes a cult to start? How to identify if you, yes you, are in a cult right now, and how to escape any cult that you could be in. Although I use my Exclusive Brethren experience as my reference, because I can, my heart is for the freedom of all who are trapped in religious cults. There are millions of people right now who are suffering in silence, fear and ignorance, whose souls and lives are under the control of a leader and a system who claim to be 'right.' They all claim to be 'right.'

Final note
This book will show that no matter how trapped, how upset and how damaged you might feel today, there is hope for you. The past does not equal the future. My journey to freedom was unique to me but has principles that can apply directly to your situation.

My desire and prayer is, that the talons of man's lust for control and power, that have wounded, scarred and destroyed so many families, marriages and individuals, would be exposed for what they truly are. Then new hope will emerge, and the hearts of the fathers and mothers will be turned back to the children, and the hearts of the children will be turned back to their fathers and mothers.

IN

Chapter 1

"*A remote control. What is that?*"

"A remote control. What is that?" I asked the shop assistant? It looked to me like a futuristic tool for a space craft. Fortunately, there was only a few buttons I had to master. On/Off, Programme, Volume and Mute.

Nowadays, three-year olds know how to operate a television. I was 22 when I was first exposed to this modern world and the 'pipeline of filth,' which is what we were told a TV was. I had just escaped from the Exclusive Brethren cult. It was 1988 and I was to enter another world of media, sport, music and entertainment; things which we had been taught were evil and of the devil.

I remember walking into my first restaurant, Uncle Sam's on Renshaw Street, Liverpool. I had no idea what was about to happen. I was approached by a friendly waiter who asked me how many of me was there. "Just me," I said, looking behind me just in case. He led me to a table and pulled a chair out for me. "Is this alright?" he asked. "It's fine," I said, coughing as the smoke from a couple on the next table filled my lungs. As I looked around, I realised that what I was doing was normal to everyone else, but to me, it was like going to a very foreign country for the first time.

I had heard of menus before but had never seen one. There was so much choice. I had been used to meat and three veg all my life and here was a huge selection of food called starters, mains and desserts to choose from. I went for corn on the cob with butter, Polla Alla Crema and a banana dessert loaded with cream and fruit. Then I just sat there being waited on hand and foot.

I remember a tramp looked through the window at me. What was he thinking I thought? Has he ever been in a restaurant? I felt quite posh actually. I was dining, I was eating in the same room as 'worldly' people and I wouldn't have to do the dishes.

My previous 22 years seemed like light years away from where I was now, even though a few days before, I had been sitting in an Exclusive Brethren meeting, my escape route on the verge of being put into action. Born into the closed confinements of a religious group that enforced a 'separation from evil' doctrine, I had embarked on an adventure of a life time, had now been cut off from all my family and friends, had risked everything in the pursuit of freedom and expressing the 'me' inside, that wanted to get out and live. It felt amazing.

When you take a child and train him up into an extreme belief system which continues the family tradition, teach him that everyone apart from us is wrong, we alone are right, create a 'them and us' culture so that you don't fit in anywhere, apart from members of your group, shower with approval when you conform, groom you to believe that the leader is to be revered and obeyed else you may be ostracised and never see your family again, you end up with a child like me.

I grew up into a clone of the dictates of a man who didn't know me, had never met me, but insisted that his 45,000 followers should conform to his laws, rules and regulations. Dare to cross the line and all remaining members were told to separate themselves from you and have nothing more to do with you, for life, unless you came under the laws again. His laws were always changing. Whenever they did, the justification was that 'god had turned a corner.' Without question, questioning was forbidden too, we all swallowed his hallowed instructions, hook, line and sinker.

I once saw 'Our Beloved Brother,' 'the Man of God,' 'The Leader of the Recovery of the Truth', 'the Elect Vessel.' I was eleven and my Dad and I were invited to an evening meeting in Sheffield. It was the same day that I had seen Queen Elizabeth on her Jubilee visit to Liverpool in 1977. That day, as I told people, I had seen the Queen and the King.

About 500 invited members sat silently for an hour waiting for him to arrive. I can't tell you the excitement I felt. How privileged I was! He was a pig farmer from Neche, North Dakota, infirm in his latter years. He arrived in a wheel chair and for an hour I sat transfixed as I saw a man who I was groomed to believe was the Universal Leader, the spiritual descendant of Paul the Apostle, wield his power and authority. The atmosphere was thick with reverence and I believe that if he had told us to all commit suicide, we would not have hesitated. He didn't go that far but the separating of families that he preached and enforced, to me is on the same level, as I know what it is like for my family to be separated by cultic law. My family was to be destroyed by his laws.

Little did I know that many gurus, teachers and leaders of many religions are also revered and followed, no matter what they decide their followers should do. I didn't know that 40,000 religious denominations all have one thing in common. They are all 'right.' I didn't know that the rules system that I grew up under meant that over half of all families were split through his laws. I didn't know that thirty years later, I would be writing a book and a resource creating awareness of what can happen if you were to join a religious cult.

I must say, this whole subject is not all grim news. In fact, it is far more about the joy of awakening to the reality that freedom is for anyone who pursues it. The freedom to live and love all, without that wretched judgement of one another, yes, learn about avoiding some of the minefields in this life, but mostly about getting our broken wings healed and learning to fly then soar, then able to see just how beautiful this world really is, with people who all really want the same thing; love.

In this first chapter I just wanted to give a flavour of what it was like for me, incarcerated by a man's religion, but then venturing out into the 'big, bad wonderful world' for the first time. The rest of the book goes into the graphic details, some gory, some shocking, some just weird, but mixed in with parents who loved me, the struggle to escape, some massive life lessons, and an ending that is all we need.

Chapter 2

A Historic Overview of the Exclusive Brethren

In 1827, a group of disillusioned Christian people started meeting in houses in Dublin. They were protesting against the Protestant Church over what they felt was jealous sectarian isolation. They became known as Brethren and they met to have communion and pray.

In the early 1830s, they were joined by an Anglo-Irish Bible teacher called John Nelson Darby. Ordained as a curate in the Church of Ireland, Darby became disillusioned with what he saw as 'the church in ruins.' Darby was the first prominent leader of the Brethren and he began to form new assemblies in Ireland and England. The first meeting in England was held in December 1831 in Plymouth and those who met subsequently became known as the Plymouth Brethren. In 1848, following a major dispute over doctrine, those who continued to follow Darby separated themselves from all other Brethren and eventually became known as the Exclusive Brethren. Since then divisions have continued to divide the whole Brethren movement into many splinter groups worldwide.

The central teaching of JN Darby and the Exclusive Brethren was his 'separation from evil, God's principle of unity' teaching. Whoever was the current leader decided what his latest definition of evil was and decreed it as law to every member. A time came when if the current law was disobeyed then that 'wicked person', was cut off from their family and excommunicated till they conformed once more to the law.

Those who didn't might never see their family again. Growing up, I was taught that such a person was to be treated like a leper in the Old Testament, that is isolated, until a priest deemed them clean.

Darby began to attract followers who subscribed to his particular interpretation of the Bible and the Brethren movement spread worldwide. After the death of Darby in 1882, one of the followers who continued Darby's particular doctrines was a man called FE Raven from Greenwich, England, who took over the leadership. These leaders had sole authority over their followers who looked upon them as being the spiritual descendants of Paul the Apostle.

More schisms formed during the leadership of Raven until his death in 1903 when the 'baton' was passed to James Taylor Senior from New York. He was to lead and introduce his interpretations and rules until his death in 1953. At this point there was a six-year gap of leadership due to controversy within the organisation, as to who should be the next leader. Eventually, his son, James Taylor Junior, also from New York took over in 1959 and was recognised as the Universal Leader. Other titles were used as I believe they are to this day, such as, 'The Leader of the Recovery of the Truth', 'The Man of God', and the 'Elect Vessel'. Again, new schisms, new definitions of evil and new rules were enforced.

In 1970, the year James Taylor Junior died, there was a major split following his apparent involvement in a drunken sex scandal in Aberdeen, Scotland where he was holding three-day meetings. He claimed that it was just a deliberate ploy to find out who his true followers were and gave the following ultimatum to all the members, 'Are you with me or against me?' About 45,000 remained with him including my parents. The rest left with some starting up new brands of Brethrenism. To this day they all observe differing levels of separation, yet all maintain that their way is the 'right' way. In my family, all our relatives who left at the split in 1970 were instantly cut off from our lives. This included my four grandparents and all my uncles, aunts and cousins.

This family division took place when I was four. I remember the Liverpool members, about 200, assembling one evening to give their personal verdict. All the adults were asked in turn if they were for or against 'our beloved brother Mr Jim.' Those who declared they were not with the 'Man of God' got up and walked out. I remember my grandfather, Harold Spinks getting up and walking out with my grandmother. He never saw me again.

The next leader was James H. Symington, a pig farmer from Neche, North Dakota who ruled till his death in 1987. Then John S. Hales from Sydney Australia ruled till 2002 by which time I had left.

Today, the group exist under a different name, the Plymouth Brethren Christian Church, the leader being Bruce Hales from Sydney, the son of John S. Hales. Has this group carried on any of the practices and kept any of the laws of their past leaders? You will have to ask them.

Today 'Brethrenism' with its many schisms consists of as many as 2.5 million attendees in 25,000 congregations in 70 countries. Many such groups are generally referred to as the Open Brethren. These tend to be more tolerant as to who they allow into their fellowship and their rules aren't as restrictive as the Exclusive Brethren's rules were. Since 1848 divisions have caused a wide diversity in beliefs and practices but one common characteristic that they all share is that they all think that they are the right group, assembly, position or church.

So it was the particular strand of Exclusive Brethren, sometimes called the Darby Raven Taylor Brethren, that I was born into.

Chapter 3

The Laws That Controlled Me

Law definition:
The system of rules which a particular country or community recognizes as regulating the actions of its members and which it may enforce by the imposition of penalties. (Google definition)

The primary purpose of this chapter is to illustrate what can happen if you join a religious cult. All have their particular controlling laws and rules. This chapter is about the ones I grew up under.

Over the years I have had many a conversation with people asking me about my life growing up in the Exclusive Brethren. One of the main questions people are curious about is what were the laws/rules that we had to abide by?

First of all, why were there laws and who did they come from? The Exclusive Brethren's identity was rooted in a very extreme core doctrine that originated from their first prominent leader, J. N. Darby. In 1847 he established this doctrine in a pamphlet titled Separation from Evil, God's Principle of Unity. It is not unreasonable to state that this pamphlet and associated doctrine was the very ethos on which Exclusive Brethrenism hung. All rules originated from how we were to be separated from what the leader deemed as evil.

As a child, we never questioned the rules or even the new ones that came out on a regular basis. Looking back, I suspect the adults didn't either. Perhaps when people who from birth are following a man, (whom they are indoctrinated into believing that they should completely submit to his control over their lives) they find it totally normal to just sit back and let him dictate whatever he reckons God has told him to say and do. Why should we know more than him? When a rule changed, that having a cat or dog, for example, was good one minute but changed to evil the next minute, here was what the Man of God said to justify the radical change.

'God has turned a corner.'

We all believed this because we were told to.

The rules were for the purpose of maintaining the 'separation from evil' doctrine as decided by the Man of God. The rules changed as and when he decided they did. When they changed, the members worldwide meekly submitted no matter what they were. Whatever he said became instant law.

Here are some of the rules that we had to obey when I was a member during the first 22 years of my life. To break any of these rules would mean instant 'assembly discipline,' which is explained in the Chapter on Breaking the Rules.

I have gone into fine detail because I wanted to illustrate just how controlling some cultic groups are and just how much they can take over their member's lives.

Houses must be separate.
In 1984, the Man of God, JH Symington, an American living in Neche, North Dakota decided that if your house had shared drains, driveways, or adjoining walls you were not considered separate from evil anymore, so you had to move house. We loved our family home. I was born there, and it contained most of our happy childhood memories. It was in the leafy Wavertree Garden Suburb, Liverpool with playing fields at the back, gardens front and back and had many great amenities. We were sad to have to leave but within a year the house was sold, and we moved into an end terrace house a mile away in Mossley Hill. This house had no gardens, was smaller and the move was a great inconvenience for my parents. However, rules had to be obeyed without question.

Houses must be even more separate.

About a year later, Symington decided that end terraces, even if they did have separate drains, driveways and no adjoining walls, were not separate enough, so we had to move again. Now only detached houses were deemed as being separate enough.

I remember hearing of an Exclusive Brethren farmer in the South of England who had a stone wall all the way around his farm. The wall was jointly owned by him and his neighbours. He got permission from Symington and the agreement of his surrounding neighbours to cut a fine slit down the middle of this wall using special equipment. Now he was considered 'separate' enough.

All contact with anyone who had been excommunicated was strictly forbidden.

Once a person had been withdrawn from, or even shut up, they were considered unclean and we had to keep away from them. I found the following scenario that happened many times really weird and disturbing. We all knew Bill and his family very well. We saw them all many times a week at the meetings and had been in each other's homes for meals many times throughout the years. One evening meeting there was an 'issue'. This was always very exciting for us children as it broke the monotony of the typical mundane normal meetings. The issue was that Bill had misrepresented the Man of God by making a decision on a 'priestly' matter without fully understanding the Man of God's instructions. It was called the sin of presumption and he was to be withdrawn from with immediate effect. At the meeting that night the issue was brought up and the fatal words were spoken which always were, 'We can no longer walk with our Brother so and so.' All would say, 'Amen,' I remember Bill walking out of the room his head hanging down. He was to get an apartment away from his wife and children. In his case, he was restored about a year later if I remember rightly.

Anyway, back to the point. The day after Bill was withdrawn from, I saw him walking towards me along Allerton Road by the shops. From being a great familiar friend up to the evening before, I was filled with fear and dread as this 'unclean' man was walking towards me. I immediately crossed the road feeling very shaken.

No marrying anyone unless they are a member of the EB.

This rule meant that there was always a potential shortage of appropriate spouses. There were many bachelors and spinsters in the EB who never found the one they wanted to marry, and I reckon it was because they were restricted in their choice. I was one of them and I am thankful I didn't get married in the EB. The reason for this is that once a person is married, it is far more difficult to escape because of the terrible consequences of leaving your spouse, children, parents, in-laws, and other relatives behind.

All marriages had to take place on a Tuesday evening and the couple had to be married by one of the male EB members who was registered to marry. All marriages took place in one of their meeting rooms. Wedding receptions were not allowed, and the bride could only wear a white dress. An old rule was that once married, the man and wife had to always sit next to each other whenever they had a meal.

From my perspective, one of the greatest strengths of this group of people was, and is, that they believe, see and think that marriage is for life. Because they had no television, they were not constantly bombarded with images of divorce and marital separation, and so were not being constantly fed with the 'normality' of marital breakdown. Divorce among the EB was virtually unheard of.

I suppose ultimately, I can only speak from my experience of my parents whose life and marriage was always in front of me. My Dad loved my Mum and she submitted to him in a way that made them one, and a team that always worked together in beautiful harmony. I never heard a harsh word spoken between them and it taught me how marriage can be. Years after leaving the EB I was to discover a passion inside me which is to help marriages and create a career in doing so. Maybe a seed was sown in those years with my parents and the example of marriage that I was shown by them both.

Couples could not hold hands when engaged to be married.

Looking back, I remember courting couples after the meetings just standing together but keeping their distance which even then did seem a bit odd. People were strongly encouraged to marry as young as possible and most did. I remember going to a wedding in Chester. The groom was 16 and his bride 18.

Funerals: Not all 'out of fellowship' relatives were informed of a death.

Like most areas of the EB, rules change over the years. Most of the following applied when I was there. The authorities let the EB bury their own dead. In Liverpool, they had access to their own hearse and were registered to administer their own funerals. Surprisingly, members were buried in public graveyards alongside 'worldly' bodies. They were never cremated. Those who died had to be buried in the same area where they die, and the body had to be in a house before the burial. A funeral service was held at the EB meeting room before the burial, usually early in the morning so members could get to work afterwards. The coffin was placed in the middle of the meeting room and was open for all to see. They had three short addresses then everyone walked past the body. I remember as a child seeing lots of dead bodies, about forty I reckon. I remember seeing a few with snot up their noses, their eyebrows seemed to be accentuated and a few of them gave me nightmares. One was an old man who was whiter than usual and to me looked like a ghost. Another was an old lady who I had seen a month before. She had always been very large and rotund. In the coffin, she had shrivelled to a tiny body and I didn't recognise her. More nightmares.

If someone died who was not an EB member, but whose next of kin was, the funeral service was not allowed to be in an EB meeting room. Relatives who were not in the EB were not welcome, (welcome means to be gladly received), at burials or marriages and were told to keep apart at the cemetery if they happened to go.

A family I personally know left the EB in the 1980s. The father's mother, who stayed in the EB, died but he was not told about her death till three months after she was buried. I cannot think of a crueler and more inhumane act, and to this day, as far as I am aware from the family, they have not put that matter right.

All were to attend the daily meetings.
Some of the rules were unspoken. Everybody was expected to attend every meeting unless they were ill. There was one meeting every single day, 365 days a year, apart from Sunday when there were five meetings, with the first one starting at 6 am.
Meeting rooms had to be separate from a house, presumably in case the household got shut up or withdrawn from. No clocks or mirrors were allowed in the room and a later rule was that digital watches were also banned. Owning a mobile phone was strictly forbidden so at that time they didn't even come into the equation. Also, no food or drink

was allowed in the meetings although apparently, Jim Taylor used to have a glass of whisky under his seat, but then he was the Man of God! I remember the many times I, and no doubt many, were desperately thirsty especially in the warm weather.

Each meeting lasted about an hour. All seating was in concentric circles with only the men sitting on the front rows. The women all had to sit separately in the back rows and were not allowed to speak during any meeting. Only the men did the talking and there was a time when only married men were allowed to read the scriptures.

The norm was that meetings always started with a hymn which always had to be sung sitting down. Only the women could give out a hymn but only a man could start the singing. An older rule was that you were not meant to look around whilst singing. There was a special hymnbook with only hymns that the Man of God accepted. The only Bible allowed to be used was the translation by the founder of the Exclusive Brethren, JN Darby. Note-taking was not allowed during the meetings. On a Sunday, men wore white shirts and no jeans but Monday to Saturday wore a coloured shirt and jeans if coming to/from work.

I grew up going to eleven meetings a week. There was a rhythm which our lives just fitted around. Every Monday to Friday the meetings were 7.45 pm so after our evening meal it was always, "time to get ready for the meeting now". The Saturday meeting was 10 am apart from once a month when it was 6 am. On these early morning Saturdays, we had all day to go out to the beach or the countryside etc though we had to be back to get an early night for the Sunday morning meeting.

The Sunday 6 o'clock in the morning meeting.

For 52 weeks a year, we all had to attend what was called the Lord's Supper or The Breaking of Bread. More traditional churches call this the Communion Service. Years ago, it had been at 9 am until one of the Men of God decided to change it to 6 am. Although this early morning start was 'normal,' to us all, it was still a chore to have to get up, and half asleep, go through the motions and the rituals. There were lots of specific rules surrounding this meeting which saw lots of changes too over the years, as each Man of God decided how they wanted it done. Here are some of them.

We were not to have breakfast before this meeting. When we arrived, there was always a solemn atmosphere like a funeral, partly because we were not allowed to greet one another before this meeting. Only a woman could lay the communion table and it had to be with a linen cloth. A woman had to make the loaf of bread which was always white. The wine cup had to be uncovered and both the cup and the bread had to placed away from the money basket. Children, at this time in EB history, were allowed to take the bread and the wine. These had to be handed to the women first and a woman had to take them out at the end and finish the wine if there was any left.

We always had Cockburn's Port and us young ones always hoped that we would be the last one to get the cup. This is so we could finish it off and many times over the years it was me. Provided there were no soggy crumbs in the cup I would often get about five full gulps down before I started getting scowls. I would then spend the rest of the meeting with my head spinning as port on an empty stomach of anyone would have that effect, including a small child.

No watching, listening or even physically touching a television, radio at home or in a car, computers or pre-recorded music.

These items were all categorically forbidden whilst I was in the EB. A television was called a "pipeline of filth". These were all "instruments of the world". All cars bought by EB members had the radios and aerials removed. In 1982 when Charles and Diana got married, a third of the Brethren were 'shut up' for seven days because they somehow managed to see the royal wedding on a television. One person was cross-examined as to whether his visit to the chip shop, where the highlights of the wedding were being shown, constituted him seeing it or not. The issue was, did he go there for the chips or the wedding? After much deliberation, which took about 20 minutes, his plea that chips were the motive, was thrown out and his whole family was disciplined for seven days.

From the age of 16, I used to sneak into Liverpool city centre as often as possible on my own and watch TV in one of the many shops. I cannot tell you how exciting it was for me. I would stand watching for about half an hour then move to another shop, so it didn't look suspicious. I remember watching Ian Rush and Liverpool beating Everton in two Cup Finals, Boris Becker winning his first Wimbledon, probably the whole series of Dallas and many, many more programmes. I watched Charlie Chaplin in The Circus and remember laughing till tears rolled down my face. Then one day a new issue came out from the Man of God. Anyone who had physically touched a "pipeline of filth" had to confess it. So, I confessed my 'sin' of turning the volume up and two 'priests' came around to see me. I told them that I had been watching TV in shops where I had changed the channels and turned up the volume many times. They deemed me to be repentant, so nothing happened to me on that occasion. On Saturdays during the football season, I would make an excuse to go down to the shops at about 4.30 pm. I would stand in front of a TV shop window watching the football scores come in live. Compared to the stifling boredom of the meetings, television was thrilling even if I was watching it outside whatever the weather.

No mobile phones or radio-controlled gadgets or toys.
We were told that Satan was the "god of the air" so it was considered worldly to use anything that was in his domain. In the mid-1980s, the Man of God instigated a season of confessing a new raft of 'sins' which had been largely ignored but were now considered definitely evil. The Tuesday evening meeting was the usual 'issue' meeting and one such evening anyone who had previously used anything radio controlled had to confess their 'sin.' Not really sure what this included, people started confessing to using radio-controlled toy cars, toy aeroplanes and garage doors. Someone confessed to having radio-controlled window blinds but the one us children enjoyed the most was a confession of a very timid old lady. Bearing in mind women never spoke except to give out hymn numbers, hearing a female voice through a microphone was a great novelty. With a small voice quivering with great embarrassment she confessed to the hushed assembly that she had been using a cordless kettle. In fairness, we were all technophobes but most of knew that cordless kettles were not radio-controlled.

No 'worldly entertainment' including any sporting event, going to the cinema or theatre.
On a fairly regular basis, you would hear someone in the meetings refer to the "The World of Sport". I remember this always being said with severe condemnation, for this wicked entertainment that would beguile and entice any of us into the "present evil world," if we dared to even look. In saying that, children were allowed to have posters on their bedroom wall and collect football stickers. We were also allowed the Daily Telegraph newspaper and for years I would run downstairs each morning to eagerly read all about the sport from the day before. Whenever Liverpool FC used to bring home a trophy, which was most years, I would sneak out and watch their homecoming processions and see the trophies they held up at the front of the bus. When I could drive, I went to their training ground and got the autographs of the team

including Bob Paisley, Kenny Dalglish, Phil Thompson, Ian Rush, John Barnes, Bruce Grobelaar, Alan Hansen and many more.

No going to funfairs or theme parks.

One of the most exciting times for a child is the Roller Coaster, the Ferris Wheel, the Haunted House, The Waltzers and all the rides and fun of the fair. These places were strictly forbidden. We could go to zoos though and many times we would go to Southport Zoo. By the entrance was also the entrance to the Southport Funfair. I remember how I, and no doubt my brothers felt as we walked past and had a glimpse of inside. We could see happy children, the colours, the candy floss, hear the screams on the rides, smell the doughnuts and the burgers and sense the great excitement in the air. I remember feeling so sad and had a great longing to just run in and enjoy myself with all the other children.

Having any pet is forbidden.

In 1964 JT Junior banned all pets. Brethren had to somehow get rid of them or get them put down. I know two people whose dogs were put down the very next day. They were seen as a distraction from giving our affections to God. Thousands of parents had to explain to their children that having a pet was now evil and worldly and how they had to separate themselves from these animals. Dogs, cats, hamsters, fish, gerbils, all had to go or be killed. Having them was now evil for God had "turned his corner" again. I was born after this rule was introduced so grew up not knowing what it was like to have a pet. When I was 15, I bred rabbits for two years. This was allowed as it was considered commercial. I started with a pedigree Californian buck, called Cali and over the two years, he had nine wives and 210 children. I used to sell the baby rabbits to a local pet shop on Wavertree High Street for a pound each. I wonder if pets are still banned?

No going on holiday home or abroad.

Having to attend the local meetings each day meant there was no time to go on holiday, so we never did. We were restricted to day trips within a few hours' drive. We could go on walks, visit museums, art galleries, beaches and the like. A common day out for us was the beach at New Brighton, Wirral. We would pack the car with deck chairs, a picnic with sandwich spread sandwiches, towels, buckets and spades and set out to drive through the Mersey Tunnel. New Brighton always felt like freedom to me. We spent many happy childhood days on that beach doing what children do best. However, there was always a concern; the dreaded radio or music that someone would be playing on the beach. To keep separate we were expected to be at least 100 yards from the nearest people which often meant moving our pitch so that the sound of the world wouldn't be in our ears.

Not long after I had escaped these restrictions, I took my first holiday to El Arenal in Majorca in the Balearic Islands. I was able to experience the wonderful world that I had been missing; swimming in a warm turquoise sea, Mediterranean sun, fine food, dancing the night away, meeting new people, forgiving the Germans for taking all the sunbeds and topless German women with hairy armpits on the beach. What a wicked world!

No going into a 'worldly' neighbour's house.

There was a sort of despising fear about worldly peoples' houses. They were so alien to us. For a start, they had a TV on all the time and some of the men had facial hair and some of the women wore trousers. I remember next door but one, was a Catholic family. Although we knew nothing at all about Catholicism, I remember feeling hatred for these 'stinky' people. I grew up with terrible judgments against all people that weren't like us. If you are one of those people reading this, please forgive me. My brother Andrew started calling in to a school friend's house on the way home from school for ten minutes or so. He confided in me about how amazing the music was from the 1950s and1960s that his friend played for him. The EB found out and my brother was shut up. A few months later, as soon as he turned sixteen, my brother walked out of our house and the EB never to return.

No eating under the same roof in any building where there were 'worldly' people.

I once thought that if Jesus and Paul the Apostle had been in the Exclusive Brethren, they would have had to be withdrawn from for there is rather clear evidence that Jesus and Paul ate with all manner of people under the same roof.

In Mark 2 it says, 'And it came to pass as he lay at table in his house, that many tax-gatherers and sinners lay at table with Jesus and his disciples; for they were many, and they followed him.'

Paul encouraged the following in his advice to the Corinthians, '..if any one of the unbelievers invite you, and ye are minded to go, all that is set before you eat, making no inquiry for conscience sake.'

One day, the rule changed. Eating with anyone, even Christians who were not EB members, became evil. This law was introduced around 1960 by the then Man of God, James Taylor Junior and we can only wonder at the significant detrimental impact this would have had on people's lives.

We were used to it of course. It was 'normal' for us to never go into, let alone eat, in a pub, bar, hotel, restaurant, cafe and literally any place where there was a roof and a 'worldly' person. This obviously included not having a cup of tea with a neighbour. In school, we had to come home for dinner every single day as we were not allowed school dinners with others. Where EB members worked, they had to eat separately.

No attending school assemblies or having Religious Education.

I never attended the morning school assembly in the eleven years I was in school. I stood outside the hall doors as the whole school walked past me. I remember at the age of eleven looking through the hall door window at the 1200 children all facing the stage. I had this thought. 'Why me? Why is it that I have the truth and all these children are deceived?!' Ouch! I felt different and separate from the other children. I was not allowed to have Religious Education either and had to sit outside the class reading a book. The EB did not want us exposed to any other teaching or alternative opinion. The only religious books we were allowed to read were JN Darby's translation of the Bible and the many volumes of books which were transcribed from the meetings and the writings of the Men of God. We had the complete package of truth, the only right position on earth, and to cap it all, we had the Universal Leader!

No visiting other churches.

It would be unthinkable to even visit another church apart from the fact we had our own five meetings to attend each Sunday. Since we never had any conversations about religious things apart from the EB meetings, my viewpoint was totally blinkered. The only other 'churches' that I knew the name of was Protestant, Catholic, Baptist and Methodist. I was shocked later when I learnt that there are over 40,000 denominations.

No going to University or taking Advanced levels.

At that time, Further Education was seen as a danger to young people growing up in the EB. I was aware that the viewpoint would take us away from the sanctity and sterile safety of their eleven meetings a week lifestyle, and they feared that teenage members would be exposed to alternative beliefs and ideologies.

Looking back, I realise that my parents didn't push me to excel in my exams and now I understand why. The hope was that I would get a job working for the Brethren or would start my own business in which I would not need qualifications. Naturally, I am very goal orientated but having no good reason to work hard for my exams, I found those last five school years very boring. I remember thinking 'what is the point of swotting for the ten 'O' Levels when they will have no future purpose?' So, I decided to just get Maths and English and mess around in school and have a laugh instead and get through the boredom that way. I reckon our ethos had a bonsai tree effect on myself and all the children growing up in the EB. The opportunity of excelling and achieving our full potential, and subsequently going on to careers that potentially could have made a great contribution to society, was severely stunted.

I was not to allowed to do Jury service.

When I was eighteen, I was called up to do jury service. I would have gladly gone but the EB told me that I was not allowed to, as it would involve making joint decisions with worldly people. Separation from the EB Man of God's versions of evil, was the root of all decisions, as was this one.

All must have the photos of the 'Men of God' on their lounge walls.

On every lounge wall in every household, there were a set of photographs of all the Men of God, known as 'Leaders of the Recovery.' These men were revered, titled and were the sole rudders that have steered the changing doctrines of separation from evil. I remember often wondering why JN Darby had thick sideburns, FE Raven had a thick beard and large moustache and James Taylor Senior had a moustache and a dicky bow. That 'worldly' appearance would have got you withdrawn from when I was in the EB. Mind you, when we all get to heaven, we might find that Peter, James and John all had short back and sides!

All over the age of 18 subscribe to weekly 'ministry' books from the 'Man of God.'

If you were to go into any EB house, you would soon see a large bookcase with hundreds of volumes of books all colour coded. These books consist of all the writings and recorded meetings taken by the leaders since, and including, JN Darby. In the EB meetings, these 'ministries' are referred to just as much as the Bible and they are part of the complete saturation of indoctrination that must be followed. Each Monday night, the latest ministry would be delivered through every EB letterbox worldwide, which was the previous week's word spoken by the Man of God.

No joining of trade unions, any unions or having a job where you must sign the Secrecy Act.

My father worked in the Midland bank for twenty years until at some point this new rule was brought in by a pig farmer in South Dakota whom he had never spoken to. Symington, the then leader, had the power over thousands of EB who instantly had to hand in their notice and quit their careers. Whilst this created huge difficulties for my father who was happy in his secure job, he obeyed without question.

Men were forbidden from having long hair, beards and moustaches.

Rules also extended to our physical appearance and we had to all conform to strict codes of hair length with absolutely no facial hair including sideburns. At some point, males were not allowed to use a worldly barber to cut their hair.

Since every single lounge wall in every EB house had photographs of all the Men of God since JN Darby, I often wondered why it was that JN Darby had massive sideburns and FE Raven had a large full beard. "God has turned a corner", was the standard reply.

Rules for women's appearance.

Women were not allowed to have their hair cut. Their hair was not to be tied up but left loose and covered with a headscarf at every meeting and whenever they left the house. For a time, the girls were forced to wear them in school too. Then that rule was relaxed whereby they only had to wear a token-like ribbon in their hair outside the house, but still a headscarf for the meetings. Trousers were forbidden as was make-up and jewelry. Tattoos or piercings were unthinkable.

The following is a list of other rules, mostly introduced by James Taylor Junior, the EB's 4th Man of God. Not all of these rules were operating in my time in the EB and all those who were in the EB in that era will recognise that over the years, they were modified or changed completely.

What is worth pointing out here is that the Man of God's definition of evil changed over the years. A rule that once caused the split of a family, later was changed, so what was used to be seen as 'sin' now became acceptable. Therefore, if those who committed the then forbidden 'evil' offence, and who had been withdrawn from because of it, had done the same thing when the Man of God has called that 'offence' acceptable and pure, then that person would have remained an EB member and their family would not have been split.

A specific example is an old friend who got cut off from his family for having a mobile phone. Mobile phones were 'worldly' and strictly forbidden. Years later, however, the law was changed. God 'turned a corner' and all of a sudden owning a mobile phone was good and acceptable.

Other Rules.

1. Children not allowed to leave home and live elsewhere.
2. Young people to meet prospective partners at EB '3-day meetings.'
3. Children banned from using computers at school lest they be corrupted by their 'satanic influence'.
4. Computer technology called "the work of the Devil"
5. Children must refer to their natural Father as "Father" rather than "Daddy."
6. The husband must be the one generally directing the conversation in the home.
7. Wives not allowed to work.
8. Women must be silent in the meetings and cannot pray or take part in the discussions.
9. The elderly must be cared for in houses rather than by the state wherever possible.
10. There was an era where women had to do feet-washing.
11. Sabbath recognised and no work that day. (Saturdays).
12. Hymn & Scriptures to be read 3 times per day at the three meal

times.
13. Not moving house indiscriminately.
14. Not allowed to be living alone.
15. Open-air preaching every week-day in a public place.
16. Hotels not to be used.
17. Birthdays not to be commemorated. It was acceptable for children though.

18. Christmas not to be recognised though children could still have presents.
19. Commerce not brought into assembly.
20. Giving to Charities not acceptable.
21. Shutting up a person to determine a matter.
22. A man is not allowed to eat with or sleep with his wife if one of them is shut up.
23. Shopping: Not to go looking around and not on Saturdays.
24. Swimming pools banned.
25. Blood donations banned.
26. Calling the Man of God "Our beloved" and "The beloved."
27. Not travelling on boats for long distances.
28. No pension funds.
29. No joining of a professional organisation (such as medicine or law).
30. No joining of any membership that includes people outside the Exclusive Brethren.
31. No taking out life insurance.
32. No standing for political office.
33. No voting in elections but can donate to the party the Man of God decides.

I've gone into a lot of detail with this chapter, primarily to make the following point:

Religious cults control people through their laws. They all have their own peculiar laws. Many have certain laws that if people leave them, their members are forbidden from having 'normal family life' with those who have left. Their laws and therefore, they the cult, separate families. Beware!

Chapter 4

Breaking the rules

assembly discipline

Simply put, the Man of God dictated his laws and we had to obey them all. There was no room for questioning his authority for he had the last word and the final say. His laws changed according to what his current views were on what he deemed good and evil. He would say that all his judgements and disciplines were based upon the Bible. The reality was that they were based upon his interpretation of the Bible. Anybody transgressing or breaking the Man of God's interpretations of his laws were immediately subject to 'assembly discipline'. The terms they used for the discipline of a person breaking their laws was 'shut up' or 'withdrawn from'.

To be 'shut up' was to be suspended from all meetings. This could be for seven days or could go on literally for years until the EB priests believed that God had forgiven that person and deemed them worthy to return. The seven-day shutting up rule was from an ancient Jewish law from an Old Testament verse that says that lepers should be isolated for seven days until the priests have checked that they are clean.

To be 'withdrawn from' was to be excommunicated whereby all members were banned from having anything to do with you. This included being totally ostracised by members of your own family including wife, husband or children. The EB only withdrew from a member if they committed what the current Man of God believed was a serious sin and would not repent about it. To repent means to change your mind and agree with how the Man of God sees that particular 'sin'. Being withdrawn from could also mean losing your home and, if you worked for an EB company, your job.

My four grandparents, uncles and aunts, were withdrawn from when I was four. Their 'sin' was that they decided not to carry on submitting under the then Man of God, James Taylor Junior. It was 1970 and the Aberdeen scandal had just happened. My parents decided to continue following Taylor and were forbidden from having anything to do with their parents and relatives who were now 'under assembly discipline'. This action split the family causing separation.

What actually caused this family separation? It is important to note:

My parents were instructed to separate from these now unclean people. Being under 'assembly discipline', meant we now believed they were 'evil'.

Chapter 5

My School Experiences

I started Northway Infant School in Liverpool in September 1971. I was five and one of the youngest in my class. My Mum took me and when she waved goodbye, I remember thinking, 'would I ever see her again?' I would have cried but was distracted by other children who were howling as their parents left them.

My early memories were the whole school going into the assembly hall and sitting down crossed legged. We were shown a black and white cine film about smoking and its effects. I remember seeing people in hospital making terrible noises from their throats. Then I remember in a laboratory a man in a white coat poured out thick liquid tar from a pair of lungs from a dead smoker into a test tube. I also remember the film saying that just one cigarette could hook you for life. This film motivated me to never try smoking although smoking was banned anyway in the EB.

In the second year, my teacher Mr Cocker used to throw the board duster at children who talked in class. He also played catch by throwing a tennis ball around the classroom. I once asked him, 'Can I go to the toilet?' He told me he hoped I could and that the right question was, 'May, I go to the toilet.' Maybe it was him who taught me how to be pedantic.

I practised never getting into trouble at school by always having a contingency plan. In my first year of secondary school, Miss Greener the Geography teacher made the mistake of calling me silly. As a result, she got five years of me being silly in her class. One lesson, bored as usual, I whispered to everyone around me a challenge. The first one to leave the class for 20 minutes won. They agreed but I had already thought it through. I broke open a red biro and dabbed a little ink on my nose. I then raised my hand pointing to my nose and asked Miss Greener if I could go and wash my face. When I returned 20 minutes later, the winner, someone sniggered as I went back to my seat. Suspicious, Miss Greener called me to the front and asked me if I had left the room because of a bleeding nose. 'I never said I did,' I replied, 'I had red ink on my nose.' She couldn't do anything. In her lessons, I spent many hours discreetly learning and practising the Rubik Cube. I found that applying a little oil to it, made it turn much faster. I got my record down to 29 seconds. When I sat my 'O' Level paper I wrote on it, 'Miss Greener taught us none of this,' and slept for two hours. My result in Geography was a 'U'. I left school in the July of 1981 with the only two exams I tried for, Maths and English 'O' Level.

From the first day of my school life, and for the next 11 years, I had to stand outside the school morning assembly because we had to keep 'separate from the world'. The whole school would walk past me and as a child I often felt embarrassed, different, and disconnected from my classmates. Fortunately, I was quite an extrovert at school and was popular with enough friends to always have a laugh with. However, there was one boy, who from the age of about 7 to 13 had it in for me. He was in my year throughout my school life and picked up on the fact that I was different. He would call me a Jew or a Yid thinking that those words were somehow insulting to me. Though he was never violent I always felt very threatened and disturbed whenever he was around. In secondary school, an incident happened which brought this to an end. One break time he came up to me and for no reason called my Dad a 'ponce.' I'm sure he didn't know what that word meant and neither did I. However, I knew he was insulting my Dad and for the first time in school my anger rose up in me. I squared up to him and said aggressively, "I want you out now!" That meant I wanted a fight. He backed off and kept away from me from then on.

Since we could not eat under the same roof as the 'worldlies', my three brothers and I were not allowed to stay for school dinners. I had to walk home for lunchtime during the 11 years I was at school. I remember the most acute embarrassment when my class went on a day trip to Chester. I was about 8 years old. For lunch, everyone had brought sandwiches and we sat outside in one of the cathedral gardens. Under the rules of the EB, my parents were instructed to give my teacher a note regarding my lunch. The teacher read it and told me to sit about 10 yards away from my classmates to eat my sandwiches. As I ate them my classmates were all staring at me and talking about me. At that young age, I felt very disconnected. Looking back, I remember often thinking how my classmates seemed to be relaxed and carefree about life. They seemed to know who they were and able to be themselves and express themselves. They seemed to be free and enjoying their life. In contrast, I felt hemmed in with a life of laws, rules and regulations, bans, forbidden areas and restrictions. Looking back, I was one screwed up child.

One of the abiding memories was my school friends always talking about the television programmes that they had been watching. They were always talking about this thing called Coronation Street. I had no clue what it was. I managed to go through the 11 years with no one realising that I didn't have a TV. I was too embarrassed to tell them, so I would pick up their comments and talk about their programmes as though I had seen them too. At Christmas time, the primary school put on a cine film. For some reason, my parents allowed me to watch them although I suspect they didn't actually know. I remember the great excitement, definitely the highlight of my school life as I sat spellbound. I remember watching Bugsy Malone, Champ, Toby, a few Walt Disney cartoons and The Land That Time Forgot, which gave me nightmares for three nights.

I was not allowed to take part in any extra school activities so never joined the football team or took part in a play that required rehearsals after school hours. We could play football in the field behind our house with school friends and ride our bikes together but that was all we were allowed. Going into a 'worldly' home was strictly forbidden so I never invited my school friends back to mine and never saw the inside of a friend's house. We were, therefore, unable to have sleepovers or share birthday parties or Christmas parties with our school friends. We also had to be home early for tea as we had a meeting to attend each weekday night at 7.45 pm. Obviously having a girlfriend was forbidden so I had to suppress my feelings towards girls that I liked. Apart from a crush on Miss Jarvis, a History teacher, the first five girls I liked happened to all be called Debbie. Pursuing my interest in them was obviously out of the question!

Chapter 6

My Work Life

get rich now

I left school just before I turned 16. Options to work in 'the world' were very limited as I could not take up any employment where I had to work Saturdays or evenings, sign the Official Secrets Act, join a Union or be a member of any professional association.

I think it was difficult for my Dad to advise me. He had to leave his career in the bank when the new EB rules were introduced and he was struggling himself.

One day he brought a leaflet home which was a list of courses on offer in the then Childwall College of Further Education. Though we were not allowed to go to University, apparently, I could go here if I wanted. The only course that interested me was Photography. I enrolled and for the next nine months had a wonderful time learning and practising what is still a passion to this day. These were the days, back in 1983, of analogue film, Pentax K1000s, medium format Minoltas and developing and printing in a dark room.

One afternoon my tutor Phil took me to a photographers in Liverpool city centre's Hope Street called John Mills Photography. We were there to collect some paper. I reckon a pivotal moment in my life happened here.

While waiting in the reception area Phil asked me, since I loved photography so much, if I would like to apply here for a job. I asked him what it would involve. He told me I would probably have to work some Saturdays and that I would be starting right at the bottom, making the tea and sweeping the floor. Straight away I said no as I knew that I was not allowed to work Saturdays.

Looking back, the elitist indoctrination resulted in me not wanting to start anything from the bottom. I remember arrogantly wanting to start at the top with £50,000, a studio and all the equipment from day one. I can only think this was because I wasn't taught and hadn't recognised that many things in life require a lowly start which we have to work up from. In hindsight... well, we live and learn.

Phil, our photography tutor, happened to be off one day so we spent the day in the horticulture class. Since it was raining in the afternoon, instead of going outside we all sat down to watch a film being shown on the TV. This was the first television film I had ever seen. I was sixteen. The film was in black and white and it was the 1974 version of The Great Gatsby starring Robert Redford and Mia Farrow. When a person is brought up watching TV every day it might be hard to imagine the effect it can have on someone watching a film on the TV for the first time. I sat transfixed and utterly absorbed by the unfolding plot right before my eyes.

I remember the melancholy narration by Gatsby's cousin, Nick, the loneliness of standing on the pier looking across the bay, the flamboyant parties minus Gatsby, yet the talk and intrigue about him and who and what he might be. I watched the relationship between Tom and his wife, played by Mia Farrow, strain under the affair he was having. This was the first affair I had ever been exposed to. I was shocked and deeply saddened how a married couple could fight and be so distant. This was foreign to me. I saw the way Tom boasted about his mistress to Nick and then the look on his mistress's husband's face knowing that his wife was straying. My heart was pounding. I saw the way, Tom, insisting on having the married woman he wanted, accidentally kill her. My first TV death. I felt the horror, the trauma as if it was real life. I watched in awe at the controlled way Gatsby held his emotions in check and kept his composure. Maybe the iron grip that I subsequently had on my emotions was influenced here. Gatsby gave off an air of nobility and nonchalant power despite the strain he was going through. I felt I was with him going through those extreme trying times. Then the ending. The lonely serene swim in his pool. The jealous husband mistaking Gatsby for the man who killed his wife. The gunshot and the blood. I felt I had been there, as if I had been inside Gatsby's head.

For years I felt that this film had 'got under my skin.' I felt, like Gatsby, that I too had a huge secret. I had the wealth of 'the truth' yet was unable to really share it. I walked home that day on another planet, my mind saturated with the images of the film. I had related to the loneliness of a man unable to express himself, unable to express his love and in my case, because I didn't know who I was or what I really wanted. The spectre of Gatsby's death hung over me for years; thinking that all would end in a mistake, a tragedy, a scapegoat, a noble quest unattained, but, although that has happened in a couple of ways, I reject that false persona and that cursed future. I am not Gatsby. Phew!

In the last three months of college, I got a work placement in the Photography Department of the Botany Department of Liverpool University. The Head of the department was a friendly chap called Tony Tollitt. He basically showed me all the photography equipment available and gave me a free rein to do whatever I liked. Like a kid in a sweet shop, I played with Rolex Medium format cameras, Nikon and Pentax SLR's and unlimited film and paper to print in the darkroom. I was based in London Road ten minutes from the city and I used to walk down and have regular snap-happy photo excursions.

One day Tony showed me the electron microscope. Oil companies would send in samples of rocks and the microscope could see if there were any signs of oil. Tony placed a square centimetre size piece of a Primula leaf in the microscope chamber and gold plated it. On a monitor, we could see the leaf which was then magnified 20,000 times. By slowly turning the controls, we went for a walk through this incredible world that the human eye can't see apart from through an electron microscope. We were in a thick forest of what looked like Belisha Beacons; stalks with round bubbles on the top sitting on what looked like moss. Then we came across a dinosaur. Well, it was actually a mite, an armour-plated beast with large antennae. Apparently, these feed off smaller mites and they feed off smaller mites too. Tony altered the lens to get the mite in position and we took a picture.

I reckon by having my horizons broadened through my time at college, I learnt that there is another 'world' out there to explore. Yet, it was forbidden, utterly forbidden and unthinkable because it would finish my time and life with my family and friends in the EB.

When I was seventeen and a half, I started working for an EB business called TextileService. The basis I agreed to work for them was that by the time I was nineteen, I would be earning enough to save up for a mortgage on a house. They supplied the textile and clothing manufacturers mostly around the North West. For the first six months, I made ironing board padding and covers, dispensed cleaning fluid and oil into small containers and prepared orders. After six months I started delivering the products all over the North West and selling them on a commission basis. As I travelled around meeting people and experiencing different cultures, I realised that there was more to life than the enclosed and stifling regime that I had been born into.

At nineteen I gave in my notice and left TextileService as I was not earning what I had been promised. I looked in the Daily Telegraph and saw an advert saying, 'Get Rich Now, Ask Me How.' I went to a meeting in the Tickled Trout, a pub in Leyland, Lancashire and signed up to be a Herbalife distributor. Their theory was that we don't absorb all the nutrition we need because we are all clogged up with the additives, preservatives, flavourings and colourings in our food. We, therefore, need their herbs to clean our colons so that we could absorb the nutrition we needed, taking away the desire to overeat, which makes people overweight. The products were mainly aimed at the weight loss market. When I used to start something, I would throw everything I had into it until I got bored. I took their products religiously and lost 14 pounds in the first fortnight and felt great. With this impetus, I started selling their products earning a living income, and in the two years that I sold Herbalife, I recruited about fifty agents. By the end of the two years, I had realised that I was not going to make a quick million. The products, though fantastic, were too expensive for most people in the area. Also, I discovered that most people, in Merseyside anyway, didn't stick to commission only jobs. They wanted a fixed income.

When my Dad had to leave his banking career, he started selling Kleeneze products door to door.
He built up a round for five years then decided to start up his own cleaning supplies company. He offered me his Kleeneze round and I took it over. At that time, I bought my first car with a Nat West bank

loan of £3500. It was a cream Peugeot 308SR. I paid the bank loan off in the first six months then realised that this Kleeneze job wasn't going to land me a quick million, so I started more ventures. I signed up to sell NSA water filters, again finding that they were too expensive to make it into the big time. I tried manufacturing flagstones, manufacturing my own line of face and hand cream, started JD International, because I liked the name, and started importing false teeth from Japan and nick-nacks from China. I started a mail order business selling information and a leaflet delivery company. There were more crazy ideas that I tried and by the time I was twenty-one I found myself off in search of another business venture idea at a business meeting in... three guesses; the Tickled Trout.

I walked into the meeting and sat next to a tall slim blonde girl in a shimmering silver dress like Diana Ross, the dress I mean. She was single, stunning and vivacious and I found out she was to be my up-line if I signed up for the job. The job was selling L'Arome perfumes. It wasn't a difficult decision to make. These were excellent imitations that didn't fade in five minutes and were virtually identical to the real thing. The most popular were 'Giorgio of Beverley Hills, Coco Channel, and Chloe.' The samples were in little crystal bottles which fitted neatly into a smart burgundy case which I used to show prospective customers. I decided to take this case into every office in the North West that I could find, which I did, with the following pitch which was extremely successful. I would walk into a building or office and say to the receptionist, 'Hello, I wonder if you could give me your opinion on some perfume please?' Nobody ever said no. Women love to give their opinion on perfume. I left samples for the whole office and came back to collect the orders. Quite a few office blocks had a concierge at the entrance that prevented salesmen like me getting in. Necessity being the mother of invention, I would walk up to them confidently and from the notice board, listing the companies in the building, I would read the company name on the top floor. I would then ask him which floor 'that company' was on and he would let me in. I would get the lift to the top floor and work my way down via every office. When I got to the first floor, I would get the lift to the ground floor so the concierge would see me get out of the lift and it wouldn't look suspicious. I sold lots of perfume and recruited about forty other distributors but again found that most people wanted a fixed income job and weren't prepared to really put the time and effort in to make themselves and me rich. The funny thing was that in all the ventures I tried, I seriously believed I would make a quick million. I was naive, to say the least, and hyper over-optimistic but I had a lot of fun and great experiences along the way.

It was in my eighteen-month era selling L'Arome perfumes, that I was to leave the EB. During the previous three years, I had been able to travel and meet over a thousand people. I was experiencing life outside the confines of the EB. I was becoming more aware of the narrow mindedness, the judgmentalism, the despising of the 'worldlies,' the contrast to the dryness of the daily meetings, the temporary feeling of freedom from restrictions and the condemning of so-called worldly things. I was still totally indoctrinated into still believing that the EB system was the only right "position" and yet inside me, I was experiencing a dichotomy; a questioning, a conflict of making sense of what this world was all about. It's hard to put in words but maybe I was feeling like a tree that is being continually trimmed at the roots and doesn't understand why it feels that it should be growing a lot taller and faster, but it isn't.

A question I'm left with is, how much did my EB years affect my growth and development?

Chapter 7

How did it feel growing up?

we were 'right.'

I was in the 'right' religion, the 'right' church, the 'right' position, the 'right' denomination.

Everyone else was wrong, or not as 'right' as us.

We were in the best 'church' on earth. We had the truth. We were in the truth. We knew the truth about the Bible like no one else and like no other group of people. We had the direct 'spiritual descendant' of the Apostle Paul as our leader. Our leader wasn't a mere leader of a 'church' like the Pope or an Archbishop. He wasn't just the Leader of the Solar System. We had The Universal Leader. These 'facts' were my absolute truth. They didn't need to be proven or explored any more than you don't have to verify that you probably have two ears on the side of your head. We were 'separate' from all humans who, unless they were in our 'only right group', were unworthy of our fellowship and unworthy to break bread with us. (take communion/worship together)

As I have already written, I remember at the age of 11 standing outside the school assembly looking through the window. I saw the 1200 or so pupils all facing the headmaster on the stage. I actually had the following thought;

"How is it that I have the truth and all these people are deceived? How fortunate am I!"

Ouch! I remember having that vivid thought as if it was yesterday. I sigh as I write this. What a bigoted, self-righteous, judgemental, pharisaical, hypocritical legalist I was already acting like, and I was just 11 years of age!!

In my years in the EB, I felt superior to other people. I believed we had the truth; we alone had the Man of God. We knew exactly what it meant to keep ourselves "unspotted from the world". We felt we were the only group that practised separation from evil. We alone were the ones who were 'recovering the truth.' Outside the EB I never felt I fitted in which isn't a surprise. Anyone not in the EB was looked on and labelled as 'worldly,' 'out of fellowship' or 'outs.'

However, this weird separation from the 'world' was counteracted by 11 meetings a week, every day, 365/366 days a year which we all attended without fail unless we were ill. We also spent lots of time in each other's houses eating and drinking and socialising together. So, the lifestyle I grew up in felt 'normal' to me the same way in which, I believe, any cult member feels 'normal.' The familiarity of the lifestyle along with the strong need for belonging is realised in tightly-knit groups. I felt safe. I remember at the age of about 10 looking around the meeting room one evening. I looked at the old men, members of the EB since birth. These were all sober thinkers, nice people, intelligent, totally sincere and fully committed to their beliefs. These old men knew the bible text back to front. I remember thinking this exact thought. "There is no way these men can be wrong!" By the way, I also respected the women too for all wearing headscarves and 'keeping silent in church.'

The following illustrates how scared we could be, in an otherwise normal situation.

I was about 7, on a bus with my Mum, when all of a sudden, we were struck with terror. An old woman got on the bus with a machine gun and started shooting everyone.
Actually, she didn't, but I said that to illustrate the feeling of sheer terror that I had. My stomach was churning with acute fear. Why? This

woman was my great Aunt Irene who had left the EB in 1970, three years previously. This 'evil, unclean, worldly woman,' who had fallen so low as to reject 'The Man of God' was walking up the bus towards us. Fortunately, she didn't see us, and she got off before we had to. Why did I literally feel terror and acute embarrassment?

Another time someone who had been excommunicated, only the night before, was walking down the street towards me. I had known this person all my life very well but now they were 'out of fellowship' I was filled with fear. So, I crossed the road in excruciating embarrassment and dread.

How can such fear and horror grip someone in this way? Here's my view. The fear I experienced was a symptom of the indoctrination that these 'outs' were evil, wicked and unclean people. My mind had been taken over with a highly powerful concoction of the following:

1. I believed we alone had the truth.
2. My parents who loved me, who were utterly sincere, trained me up in this way.
3. I didn't know any different.
4. I grew up spending time every single day in meetings with likeminded people devoted to the same beliefs.
5. I had my 'need' for belonging fulfilled.
6. The whole Bible was interpreted from the latest perspective of the Man of God.
7. I was taught esoteric knowledge that only we knew which made us feel special.
8. I was trained to see how and why anyone leaving us was wicked and unclean.
9. I believed that my eternal security was dependent on staying in our fellowship.
10. If I left, I could lose my parents, family and the only people I knew.

These ten concrete beliefs had a vice-like grip on my mind. Being indoctrinated this way meant that my mind only ever looked at agreeing loyally and wholeheartedly with the belief system of the man we all revered and followed closely. The fear of the awful consequences of leaving kept me from ever wanting to even stray towards questioning any of what we believed.

Although my years in the EB felt 'normal' to me, since it was all I had ever known, I recognise now that there was always a deep internal conflict of values going on. This conflict and the strain of conforming and keeping rules and the bonsai tree effect on my growth and development, contributed to a life of feeling 'right', different, privileged, abnormal, superior, bored, secure, insecure, yet protected by the 'truth.'

In the last four years before I left, the boredom of the dry monotonous daily meetings, coupled with the deep desire for freedom and expression of my identity, started to increase the internal conflict of values. At the time, of course, I did not understand this. It caused me to feel unhappy as I became more and more double-minded. I felt like a rope in a tug of war. There was no way that I could leave my parents for good and potentially never see them again because I knew they would be told to separate from me. However, there was no way that I could stay suppressed, restricted and let more years of my life slip away.

Reflecting on my childhood with the upbringing I had, I see both advantages and disadvantages. The old adage is true that there are people in far worse situations than what I experienced. We can always choose to make the best with what we have today. Where it is challenging, we can put it down to learning and experience. Life can make you stronger or it can crush you. My childhood was generally a happy one because I was very blessed to look on the bright side of life. I was very fortunate to be able to choose to spend most of the time in my mind on the sunny side of the street with parents who were very loving to me.

The extreme separatist lifestyle gave me an exclusive 'I'm right' complex which has taken years to shake off. It taught me to judge everyone as unworthy of our elite company and to live with a 'them and us' attitude. This extreme viewpoint has taught me first hand just how destructive living in judgement is. It has helped me seek to go in the opposite direction and discover what happens when you accept and love everyone. I have seen how putting law and rules on people binds them up and crushes them. Again, this has helped me see how the opposite works which is unconditional love and acceptance of all.

Basically, I was brought up to judge the world through the lens of the man that we all followed and who held us under the power of his influence. I have come to see that judging with any perceived knowledge of good and evil is 'normal' and totally natural in this world. It leads to the eye for an eye, tooth for a tooth judgement. This produces the penal justice system which is the way of life for much of society. Through seeing it outworked at an extreme level I have come to see that it is only restorative justice that truly works and heals a person.

Through the Exclusive Brethren modus operandi, I have seen how law breeds more law which breeds more law and how it only conditions people, produces self-righteousness and ultimately condemns them. Unconditional love, on the other hand, releases people into realising the call of their true heart to live out the love that is innate in them and in everyone.

Chapter 8

Funny Memories

including Sandy Huckley's buns...

What people find funny or amusing tends to be relative to their culture and upbringing. What may be hilarious to one, might be offensive to another. In the solemn religious and stiff environment of the EB meetings, a basic breaking of wind could cause a fresh ripple of mirth that would be remembered and reflected on for a long time to come. However, it was only the young ones who ever had the ears to hear such bodily renditions. Anyone mature and righteous appeared to be completely oblivious.

Everybody including children were expected to attend all the meetings unless they were ill. This was eleven meetings a week, including five on a Sunday which started at 6 am. Children were expected to sit still in silence and behave themselves. Children who made noises, distracted others or misbehaved were punished by their parents after the meeting. This environment meant we grew up with an unnatural tension and a fear of getting the giggles and making a noise.

Such was the dry monotony for most of us young ones, we were always on the lookout for anything to break the boredom. The following are a few memories and funnies of such happenings, which though may sound ridiculously insignificant to you, were some of the highlights of our life of conformity, restrictions, rules and regulations.

Coping Mechanisms.

When you consider that the average attention span of an adult is twenty minutes, how would the average child cope sitting through an hour or more of theology and hearing about what the Man of God had been saying?

I ate myself.

I used to gnaw my hands, bite off the skin and suck the blood if I bit too deep. I've still got the scars. I used to get so hideously bored and I reckon most of the children did too. I used to count the tiles on the ceiling, count how many people were in the room, count how many times a word was used over ten letters long. I counted many things to break the monotony. I also made charts on who would give 'a reading' or a 'preaching' over the course of a year. Then I would compile league tables just like football tables. From the charts, I would glean lots of statistics and get immense pleasure when records were broken.

Issues.

Something we used to look forward to, usually after the Tuesday night meeting, were the 'issues.' An issue often meant someone would get 'shut up' or 'withdrawn' from. The priests dealing with a matter would bring up the issue and we would get to hear the ins and outs of a 'sin' someone had committed. Often the person who had sinned would have to walk out of the room in front of everyone, sometimes with their whole family. This was high drama to us.

In the 1980s there were three new major issues in the space of about a year. The then Man of God, Symington, the pig farmer from North Dakota, decided to enforce fresh rules. Every assembly around the world had to find out who had broken these new rules and was therefore guilty. About one-third of members got 'shut up' or 'withdrawn' from for a week for each issue that they were guilty of transgressing. In the area where we lived there were about 600 members from Liverpool, Chester, Manchester and Stockport. The three issues as I remember them were:

1. Watching the royal wedding of Charles and Diana, on TV or live in London.
2. Touching people sexually before marriage.
3. Sex with a spouse before marriage.

This was a marvelous opportunity to compile some statistics and I recorded everyone who got disciplined. From what I remember the results were that only one man managed to get a hat trick and get 'shut up' or 'withdrawn from' on all three issues. Over a hundred did the double and most were caught out on just one of the issues. My parents had a clean sheet, so we never suffered the embarrassment of having to walk out of the meeting room in front of everyone.

Failing to Keep a Straight Face.

A challenge that a lot of us children went through was not getting the giggles and making a noise. We were so repressed with the solemnity and seriousness of the library-like conditions during the eleven meetings a week. This meant many times having to force ourselves to keep a straight face if possible, during the most serious of news announcements etc.

I don't know why disasters, bad news, and mishaps can cause smirking or worse, 'the dreaded giggles,' but many of the young ones including myself had a problem in this area. I still do actually so maybe I still haven't grown up yet?

At the end of most meetings, there would be updates of news about those who were ill. There were many disasters and untimely deaths which we had to cope with by trying to keep a straight face. The EB seemed to have many such terrible happenings for some reason. I remember one such announcement at the end of a meeting that caused someone to let out an inappropriate guffaw.

'I believe your wife has had a terrible mishap, Mr Williams?' someone asked.

There was a palpable silence as Mr Williams reached for the hand microphone. This was no laughing matter. Mr Williams was an old man with a very small quivery voice. We young ones braced ourselves.

'Yes,' said Mr Williams speaking incredibly slowly, 'She rolled down the whole flight of stairs this morning, whacked her head and has a bump on her forehead the size of a golf ball.'

You could hear a pin drop when someone let out half a loud guffaw and I remember myself and my three brothers putting our heads down to our knees, red-faced and shaking as we desperately forced ourselves to maintain the imperative silence.

Look Up.

Five of the eleven meetings a week were called readings. A man, never a woman because they had to keep silent, offered or was asked to take the reading which meant reading something from the Bible and leading the conversation about it for an hour.

At the beginning of one such reading a lovely old man called Barry Smythe solemnly asked the following question that had many faces straining to keep straight:

"Has anyone got a passage that we could look up?"

The Yawn Show.

The monotony and boredom of the meetings caused me to keep alert to anything that would give even the slightest bit of amusement. For many years, our second meeting on a Sunday at nine o'clock in the morning, was at the Manchester city room at Halebarns. It was called the interchange and all six hundred members from the area would gather there for a reading. The seating layout in all the meeting rooms was concentric circles with the males sitting in the inner circle rows and the women in the outer circle rows.

One such morning I noticed something worthy of amusement. Amongst the women on the other side of the circle from where I was sitting, was a lovely lady called Martha. I noticed her yawning but like no other yawn I had ever seen. Her mouth would start to slowly open for about ten seconds and at the same time, her head would move slowly back. After these ten seconds, her mouth would be wide open, and her head would be back like a head in a dentist chair. Without putting her hand over her mouth, she would keep in this yawning position for about another seven seconds which is a long time in a public place. Then as her head came back down, her lips would purse up in a very contented sort of way. She averaged this style of yawn about ten times every morning meeting.

I noticed this a few weeks running and told my brothers and a few friends. We started sitting deliberately opposite Martha to watch the show. This was pure theatre to us. All eyes were on Martha and when we thought she was about to start there would be coughing and nudges so none of us would miss an episode. Word spread and after about ten weeks I reckoned there were fifty to seventy men and boys who deliberately came a little early to get a good seat. Even my Dad knew about it, but he didn't let on that he did. With a large audience now, there was a noticeable ripple of smirks and shakings of silent laughter every yawn. If Martha was ever not there on a Sunday morning, we would be bitterly disappointed.

Sandy Huckley's Buns.

In between the second and third meeting on a Sunday, we would all go for what was called 'The Break.' At this time the interchange was in Stockport and we would all be invited back to people's houses for a light snack. One place us young ones dreaded was Sandy Huckley's. This was because her food and cutlery were not up to the standards we were used to and which most EB maintained. One such break found our family, plus two other families all invited to Miss Huckley's. She was a spinster and no one knew her age as she refused to tell anyone. When she died, we could not wait to see her gravestone and learn her age. Her gravestone, I think, said she was eighty-eight. Anyway, we find ourselves all in Miss Huckley's lounge one Sunday. It was a good size room and with all the children there must have been about sixteen of us.

Miss Huckley came in with some homemade buns, rock buns she called them. She went around the circle and we all politely took one each. Then she went back out into the kitchen. At this point, a few of us had tried to bite into our rock buns to find they were as hard as rock, possibly because of their age. Immediately, Charlie, the oldest of one of the other families stood up, picked up the waste paper basket by the hearth and went around the circle. Sixteen rock buns were thrown into the basket and Charlie left the room.

Miss Huckley came back in and sat down and general chit chat started. All of a sudden there was a thud followed by another. Then there was another and Miss Huckley stood up to see where the noise was coming from. She had a large patio window and since the noise seemed to be coming from the garden, she went to the window followed by us children. To our surprise, we saw that the thudding were white objects hitting her back fence. They were being launched from an upstairs back bedroom window and Charlie was throwing the buns, one at a time at the garden fence. Can you imagine what Miss Huckley must have thought? Only a few minutes before she had given us all a bun and now, they were being unceremoniously hurled forcefully out of her back-bedroom window.

The Rumblings.

Every single Sunday morning, fifty-two weeks a year, we arrived at the local meeting room for the first of the day's five meetings that started at 6 am. We all arrived on empty stomachs. I was once told that we weren't allowed to have breakfast before this meeting, which was called The Breaking of Bread.

This hour-long meeting was conducted in solemnity with lots of moments of silence. It was in these silent moments that the rumblings could be heard, loud and clear. They started almost straight away but after about 15 minutes, after we had all had our swig of Cockburn's Port, then the real business of rumblings would begin. Like distant thunder, something was on the move. The Sunday morning storm was brewing.

Now to get technical about it, these rumblings were what is known as Borborygmus. This is defined as a gurgling, rumbling, or squeaking noise from the abdomen that is caused by the movement of gas through the bowels. It is also known as stomach rumbling. The plural is borborygmi.

When Cockburn's Port travels bowel-ward at 6.15 am in a room of about thirty people, average age about 75, it can cause problems for young ones. It caused us a problem. We got the giggles. We got frowned at and told off. We were victims of the dreaded yet entertaining borborygmi and there was no escape.

Overcoming Shyness.

If you suffer from shyness and you want to overcome it, you might find the following useful. Before the Sunday morning yawning show we would occasionally be a few minutes late for a meeting and would have to walk in last in front of about six hundred people. We used to find this embarrassing as often the only available seats would be the other side of the large room. It seemed like all eyes were on us for ages until we eventually got to our seats.

After this happening many times over the years, it occurred to me that there is always someone who walks in last. So, I started to watch the latecomers and became aware of what I was thinking about them. I realised that I was thinking nothing, absolutely nothing. I then realised that when we walk in last everybody is thinking the same as me which is nothing. So, if ever we were late I would flip the thought around and as I walked around the room I just kept in mind that even if people were looking at me they were thinking nothing. This cured my shyness and I apply it to most situations in life where I could be tempted to be shy.

The Christening.

When I was about seven, I smuggled a small glue bottle into the meeting filled with water. If you squeezed the bottle a fine jet of water would squirt out. When someone prays in a meeting, always a man, all the older people shut their eyes. It was during one such prayer that I took the glue bottle out of my pocket, pointed it to the ceiling and recklessly gave it a good hard squeeze. To my shock, the jet shot about twelve feet into the air and in a beautiful arc came down squarely on a man's bald head about two rows in front of me. I can't imagine what he must have thought but he immediately slapped his head and looked up. I immediately shut my eyes in prayer and slipped the bottle out of sight between my legs. No one ever knew about it.

The Open Air.

The EB had what they called 'The Open Air.' This is where a few men went to a public place regularly to preach their message by shouting it out to whoever happened to be within earshot. From what I remember, it was generally about their view on how to avoid hell and get to heaven. There was never any reference to the EB as it was a bit of an embarrassment if people asked questions about who we are. In my opinion, this is because we didn't really know our identity as it was always changing. We believed we all came from JN Darby, but the ever-changing rules made it impossible to really define who we were. We used to eat with anyone, then we didn't, we used to have pets, then we didn't, we used to share drains, then we didn't etc, etc, etc.

One example of this deserves a mention. If it wasn't so outrageous it would be funny. One Saturday afternoon, someone from Manchester, who I better hadn't mention by name, was preaching his message. A nice old lady came up to him and when he had finished, asked if she could have a word. She told him that she was interested in what he was saying and that she might like to come along to his church and hear more. Here was his instant response.

"Have you got a television?"

"It's funny you should say that," she told him. "My television is broken and, in the loft, and I haven't watched it for a few years."

"In that case, I want no more to do with you!" he responded indignantly.

The reason for his indignation was because the television held so much fear for them. It was the "pipeline of filth" and the thought of having one, even one that didn't work, was repulsive.

Every Sunday morning at 5.30 am...

I am in a deep dreamful sleep. I stir as my subconscious hears a tapping on my bedroom door.

'It's half five, time to be getting up.'

Half awake, I reply sleepily, 'Ok Dad.' I am back to sleep instantly.

Tap, tap.

'Quarter to six John, we are going in 15 minutes.'

'Ok Dad,'

Back to sleep.

Tap tap. 'Five minutes, are you ready?'

I am struggling to wake up, now knowing I will have to soon be moving fast.

'Tap, tap, tap, we are going now John.'

I leap out of bed, throw my pyjamas off. Socks, pants, trousers already placed in position get pulled on, shirt gets buttoned up at high speed, tucked into trousers, shoes forced on, one sweep of my hand through my curly hair and I'm running downstairs.

At the front door, my Mum hands me my black leather-bound JN Darby bible and my hymnbook both with my initials on in gold. 'Shhhhh' says my Dad, 'don't disturb the neighbours,' as my three brothers and I creep into the car. My Dad has already opened the driveway gates silently. The handbrake is released and we roll down the short driveway backwards and into the road before the engine is started. As we drive off, only then my Dad quietly shuts his car door. We were brought up to consider others and not disturb our neighbours.

What on earth was I doing up at this hour, 52 weeks a year every Sunday morning till I was 22 years old?

I'll tell you. A pig farmer in North Dakota, whom we had never met, instructed us to be there. If we didn't, we could lose the house, business, the only people we knew, and potentially, each other.

Unquestioned obedience to this one man ruled our life.

When I think of it now, I'm sometimes apt to smile. Might as well. What a funny life for some!

Where there's a will there's a way...

What on earth could two teenage boys be doing, around 9pm, in the dark, in the bushes in a front garden of a private house, peering through the lounge window, about 5-10 times a year?

I'll give you a clue. They were teenage Exclusive Brethren looking for an outlet to enjoy their desires that had been crushed.

Their evening meeting had finished at Allerton Road, Liverpool. They believed they were committing a big sin, but this temptation was too great. Their favourite football team was playing, and the match was on TV. They were not allowed to have a TV which was known as 'the pipeline of filth,' and watching it was utterly forbidden.

I was one of those boys and I remember the thrill of sneaking off as soon as the meeting had finished. We knew the match was on as we were allowed to read the newspaper. I remember one night witnessing David Fairclough, Liverpool's super sub, scoring the winner against St Etienne in the European Cup in 1977. After 20-30 minutes, we'd rush back to the car park, so our parents didn't suspect anything.

It was common practice for Exclusive Brethren young ones to break the laws and find a way of doing what their natural desires wanted to do. But everything had to be done in secret. I heard of young ones sneaking into football grounds, the cinema, restaurants, owning radios, mobile phones, listening to pre-recorded music, watching TV in all sorts of places.

Department stores were my favourite place as you were safe there, as the EB were unlikely to see you there. I saw Ian Rush score two goals against Everton in two Cup Finals in a Woolworths store. I remember watching Boris Becker on the way to winning his first Wimbledon in the Blacklers store. I spent hours there, the staff didn't seem to mind.

This isn't a funny memory, it's just illustrates the twisted lifestyle of many young EB who lived with a conflict of values, secretly enjoying 'normal' things in life, yet believing they were committing evil acts, Why? Because a pig farmer 3000 miles away, who had never met them said so. That's why. Don't argue, or else you'll lose your family!

Chapter 9

How I Escaped

...and onto an adventure of a lifetime

One of the most common questions I have been asked over the years is, 'How did I manage to get out of the Exclusive Brethren?'

Well, up to the age of eighteen I was a committed EB member who conformed to all the rules, went to all the meetings, toed the line, and lived a life separate from the 'world' as I was taught to. So, what changed?

It all started when I began driving and experiencing the real world; a gradual process of seeing the world I was living in, through a different lens. I liken it to prehistoric man walking into a modern city for the first time. A better analogy would be likening it to a bird in a cage that starts to realise that the door is open to another world, a world in which it can naturally spread its wings and fly. In a way all was new and I began to awake to the reality of this new paradigm of existence that I had been kept separate from. Not surprisingly, I saw a spectrum ranging from very good things to very bad things. I had been told that the 'world' was only a wicked evil place, so I was surprised to see love, freedom, authenticity, respect, compassion, kindness and joy. I saw wine, women and song in moderation and in excess. I also saw addiction, guilt, fear and selfishness. My identity and personality had been encrusted with Exclusive Brethrenism and I didn't know who I was. I saw the possibility of being me, exploring and discovering my identity, yet the psychological walls around continued to keep me a prisoner. I saw it as impossible to enter into this land of so much potential freedom, which appeared to have so much milk and honey in it.

The description here of how I got out is extreme; extremely true. The violation of the human free will is a more serious issue than, I believe, anyone realises. We are appalled at slavery, the taking of a human and controlling 'it' like an animal. It is socially unacceptable and illegal. Yet to many, the control of another by instilling religious doctrine with fearful consequences if disobeyed, all in the name of God, is what we just call religion and it gets passed off as just what people choose. However, it is more than that. It involves charismatic leaders who overpower the minds of those they are able to influence and control. What makes it more dangerous, insidiously so, is that most of these leaders are totally sincere. Like Saul of Tarsus who went around doing 'God's will', killing non-conformists to his views, these leaders of today also think they have a mandate from God. They all believe they do.

This is how I would describe my getting out of the EB using metaphor.

In my four-year struggle to leave the EB, I found myself wrestling with an elaborate stronghold. This stronghold consisted of an impenetrable high wall, a moat of unknown depth filled with vipers and scorpions, a barricade of razor barbed wire and a vast minefield of death that had been constructed around me.

The wall was the trust in what my parents and the Exclusive Brethren trained me in and coercively indoctrinated me to believe, which became ingrained in my mind, forging my lifestyle and habits. This wall was reinforced daily at each meeting, 572 meetings a year, where I would hear repeated rhetoric in the exclusive environment where the need for belonging was also met.

Over the wall, if you did happen to scale it, you could easily plunge into the moat of unknown depth filled with vipers and scorpions. This moat represented the self-righteous, bigoted, narrow-minded thinking that we were in the 'right' position, were in God's will and were going to heaven. To deny this was unthinkable as the coercive indoctrination of this was so deep and on top of it, it was all we knew.

Over this moat, you were faced with another wall, this time a wall of seemingly impenetrable razor-sharp barbed wire. This barbed wire was the fear of questioning the Man of God and any of his teachings. Just one single question and you could expect to be lacerated by the threat of being shut up or withdrawn from. Those who have ever wilfully chosen to question the Man of God experienced deep cutting wounds of rejection and cursed with labels of being a bastard and evil. Many are still scarred for life.

On the other side of this barbed wire was a vast minefield of death. Take your chances through here and one foot wrong and you might never see your wife, husband, children, father, mother, relatives, job, or house again. All you once knew could be gone in a flash.

So how did I manage to escape this man constructed fortress and live to tell the tale?

I burrowed a tunnel under the whole system until I came out into the sunshine. Because I dug the tunnel out all by myself without any help, not something I'd ideally recommend, it took me about four years before I saw the sunshine. The moment I did, I leapt towards it to freedom.

I have been using metaphor so far to describe my Exodus; there's another one! Here is my attempt to describe how I escaped from more of a literal point of view.

So, back to when I was eighteen. For the next four years, I was to keep looking at this land that was there but was out of my reach. Like Jay in the film The Great Gatsby, who night after night was standing alone on his pier, looking over the bay to the brightly lit home where the desire of his heart was married to another man, I continued to look longingly at what I sensed was freedom and life and destiny, yet it was impossible. I felt like a rope in a tug of war and as each month went by, the tug on that rope from both sides became stronger. I loved my parents with all my heart and I still do, yet the bright lights of the city were also increasing the pull. The thick high wall was still as imposing as ever, the deeply held belief of the vipers and scorpions ever-present, the barbed wire was waiting to lacerate if touched and that minefield was too terrifying to even think about.

I didn't even realise that I had been digging a tunnel for four years. It was dark in there. Each day as my mind engaged with looking at an alternative to my prison life, I had been gradually secretly hacking away at the soil of my forbidden desires and exploring what they were. They had been leading me under and out of the whole EB system, but I didn't realise it. It wasn't until my 22nd birthday on the 28th July 1988 that I broke through into the sunshine. Here is how it happened.

Before I tell, I want to draw attention to an aspect of my escape first. If you are in a group/sect/cult right now you might be thinking that my pursuit of wine, women, song, and the bright lights of the city is evidence that I was on the wrong road. In hindsight, it was not. It was the best thing I could have done. However, the way I did it wasn't the ideal way, but here's my reason/excuse. In war, just do the best you can do at the time and pick up the pieces afterwards. Have faith in Love and you won't go far wrong. Back to the escape story...

So, it was my 22nd birthday. I was standing in my bedroom on my own in 31 Plattsville Road, Mossley Hill, Liverpool; the house we moved into after our first home became 'not separate' with its drains. It was a sunny afternoon about 3 pm. I looked out of the window and saw two people below staggering along appearing to be drunk. They are having more fun than me I remember thinking. It was then I had an epiphany moment, a massive realisation, and a flash of sheer clarity. Here is what went through my mind very loudly, very clearly and most emphatically.

"In ten years from today, I am going to be 32. I am not going to spend another ten years being unhappy. I am going into the world 100% and if I ever get my head round to come back to the Exclusive Brethren then I shall, but, only if I can do it 100%. Sorry Lord, I tried to please you, but I've failed."

The moment I had the thought, I felt a wave of peace go through me. I was at least being honest with myself. I also, and this is probably crucial, had a deep, though I didn't understand it, conviction that God still loved me despite my failure. I was now off the fence, single-minded and committed to moving forward. In my mind, I had now left the Exclusive Brethren. I needed a plan to make it as easy for my parents as possible. First, I immediately set about looking for accommodation. My plan was to get a place to live, get a phone line installed for my business, get a television, video player and a radio then move out. At the same time, I would tell my parents a story to get myself withdrawn from so it wouldn't look like I was walking away from them but rather, their rules meant I would have to go.

It took me till November 7th to put all the plans in place. I rented an apartment at 75 Wellington Avenue, Wavertree off an Iraqi landlord called Hamza and bought my very own TV, video player and radio. I was so looking forward to unlimited TV, watching unlimited videos and listening to the radio in the bath and in bed. You may find it hard to imagine the excitement that this gave me. But before then, a little matter of the most difficult challenge of my life. Telling my parents.

I woke up that great and terrible Monday morning, and after breakfast told my parents that I had "been with a woman" a few times. This was intended to get myself withdrawn from. I told them that I had got an apartment and was moving out that day so that they wouldn't be 'shut up', which they would be if I stayed in their house. They were devastated. My Dad begged me to stay saying it was alright that they would be 'shut up'. My Mum cried which was the first time I had made her cry. Our three hearts were broken. It was the saddest day of my life.

I insisted that there was no way I was going to let them be 'shut up' and that I hoped to be back after a fortnight when the matter might be resolved with the EB. I only said that to try to let my parents down gently. I felt that I was murdering them right in front of my eyes. It was horrible and no human should have to go through such nonsense just because one man literally thinks he knows how to interpret the Bible.

I left and drove to my apartment. Once inside I wept for literally three hours. It felt like I had killed my loving parents and I was grief-stricken. In those three hours, I believe I went through what are known as the five stages of death. At first, I felt denial that I had done such a thing. Then I felt angry that I had been put in that impossible situation. Then I went through blaming the EB and blaming God for making the rules so difficult to follow. Then I sunk into depression which was awful until the third hour. Then I remember having this clear thought. 'I don't like this emotion. I am not going to stay in this state. I'm going to the video shop to get some comedy videos.'

I went to the video shop around the corner in Lawrence Road, became a member and hired out Faulty Towers and Laurel and Hardy. I came back, watched them, laughed, and to be honest I have been laughing ever since. I believe that I am very blessed to have gone through those five stages in three hours. I did cry once a few months later when lying in bed one night when the radio played Michael Bolton's 'How Am I Supposed to Live Without You.' I felt my parents and I were feeling those words. I remember twenty years later thinking, have I bottled up some emotions deep down that could erupt one day? However even after more than 30 years, as I write this, I reckon I was able to move into acceptance of the situation in those three hours. As the years have gone by, I recognise I have received deeper healing via an amazing dream and an understanding and application of forgiveness and unconditional love.

The priests, those given the duty of dealing with EB assembly matters, phoned me up the next day. The night before, they had made an international call to the pig farmer in North Dakota, JH Symington. You will recall from earlier chapters that he was the EB Universal Leader at the time. The reason for the phone call was that they didn't know what they should do with a 22-year-old Scouser who had been with a woman and had left home. Does that sound ridiculous to you? When man devises laws and rules, they get broken, they change, they multiply, and they create man's many religions and denominations. These end up with strife and wars and a pig farmer dictating how to deal with a young man's future, whom he had never met, and who lived over 3700 miles away!

The results were that I was only to be 'shut up!' I was so annoyed. I wanted to be withdrawn from, so I upped the stakes and said it was a few women that I had been with. That did the trick. The priests called me the next evening to say they had had a special meeting and were "no longer walking with me." I put the phone down and carried on enjoying watching the highlights of Liverpool playing Arsenal at Highbury in the replay of the League Cup. It was a great game although it ended 0-0. It has been like that between me and my parents to date. A stalemate. No progress, or has there been?

It is only with hindsight, that I can now see, that 'escaping' is definitely the word to describe what I did. At the time the internal conflict of values grew so intense, that the tug of war rope that I was battling in my mind snapped and I was free. There are many different ways people escape the prison of the cult they are in. Some walk out the front gate. Some climb over the wall and others burrow their way out through a tunnel. Some never get out and they go to the grave still worshipping 'their man', fearful of offending him.

I left the EB cult in my mind on my 22nd birthday. I left their meetings and home on 7th November that same year. I still wanted normal contact with my family but couldn't, because the EB laws meant my family had to separate themselves from me. However, the indoctrination didn't leave me straight away. Even two years later I was still feeling guilty when I touched my TV set, yet it was such an enjoyable "pipeline of filth!" All those disgusting nature programmes by David Attenborough, Scott and Charlene's worldly wedding and Cliff topping the charts with Mistletoe and Wine (sarcasm intended). I still felt I was failing to please God. I made a point of not conversing with anyone about God. What was the point? I still knew the truth, so I thought; I just wasn't able to keep all the rules and regulations. Unknowingly I was still brainwashed. At least I was being honest. I was free. I was on an adventure of a lifetime.

OUT

Chapter 10

The story of my wild years

...freedom to explore the world at last!

Bonsai trees. If a bonsai tree was suddenly set free from the binds that prevent its roots from growing freely, what would happen to it? Would it launch out wildly with its newfound space to expand or would it take things cautiously. I can't speak for bonsai trees, but I can for myself. I launched out wildly and with abandon. I was like the proverbial child in a sweet shop and it was a big sweet shop. This is what I had been waiting for, for a very long time.

It took me three months to make the necessary arrangements to move out of my parent's house. This is because I was planning my life away from all I had ever known. I wanted to get an apartment and move into it and hit the ground running. I had a list of pleasures that I was longing to enjoy despite still believing they were evil. For starters; the 'pipeline of filth,' a television set. It would be a large 21-inch screen (it was 1988) and a long play video cassette recorder. I would be able to watch unlimited TV and I could hire out unlimited videos from the video shop. Then there was the radio. I would be able to listen to music and conversations while having a bath, while in bed, and first thing in the morning. I bought a cassette tape player and a record player. Music included Lionel Ritchie, Abba, Roxette, Phil Collins and of course The Beatles.

OUT

The day after I moved into my apartment, Scott and Charlene got married in the Australian soap Neighbours. Great timing! Who can forget Mrs Mangle and Suddenly, that great wedding song by Angry Anderson? Remember the last line, 'Suddenly every part of me needs to know every part of you.' This is what I intended to do in this 'big bad' world. I intended to explore it all. In the first few months, I would stay up till about 3 am watching TV enjoying my freedom immensely. I remember being able to sit on my own sofa, and without worrying who might be watching me, watch programmes like Match of the Day, You Rang M'Lord? Whose Line is it Anyway? Hale and Pace, A Bit of Fry & Laurie, Bea Smith in Prisoner Cell Block H and many more. I would tape a week's worth of episodes of the soaps then watch them all at once so that I didn't have to be in suspense with four out of five cliff hangers. My favourite comedy was Absolutely on Channel 4. This was a group of mainly Scottish comedians with very dry zany humour. The only time I have ever wet myself, well, a little, was watching one of their sketches where they were confused about the tomato soup they were eating in a restaurant.

In the first year of my freedom, I used to tape Top of the Pops and make compilation videos of my favourites. I remember the enjoyment I got from listening to Missing You by Chris de Burgh, First Time by Robin Beck, Smooth Criminal by Michael Jackson, Two Hearts by Phil Collins, Downtown by Petula Clark, Especially for You by Kylie and Jason, all the Stock, Aitken, Waterman hits and many more. After the first year of being exposed to so much music for the first time in my life, my top five favourite artists or bands were The Beatles, Abba, Queen, the Bee Gees and Whitney Houston. Those were the days when they knew how to make proper music! Half kiddin ;)

If I wasn't watching TV, I was enjoying playing snooker on my six-foot table in my lounge whilst listening to my tapes and records. I created tournaments and challenges and many statistics with many records to break. I also had a dartboard and I would have competitions between my left and right hand. Though I am left-handed my right hand was more accurate. I would eat when I wanted, drink when I wanted and sleep when I wanted. I cannot fully explain the feeling of unlimited freedom with no restrictions after the 22 years of the EB. It felt like I had been locked in a suffocating prison which you had to stay in for life because outside there were 'grievous wolves waiting to tear you apart.' Well, the wolves hadn't got me yet and anyway, I always felt a deep inner peace like I was being watched over and protected. The Jesus I had been brought up to believe in hadn't left me or forsaken me.

So, after a few days of experiencing living on my own, it was time to explore. I knew nobody at all so I wandered into Liverpool City centre which we call Town. First stop was to try out a restaurant. My very first restaurant. Uncle Sam's on Renshaw Street caught my eye and I entered this new and exciting world where I was shown to my non-smoking seat by a waiter. I learnt that you are given a menu, you just tell the waiter what you want, and the food comes to you on a plate. My first dish was Polla Alla Crema which was amazing. Half a roasted chicken drenched in chicken, mushroom and wine sauce with crispy French Fries and salad. I probably had a glass of coke, as I was driving, then I ordered the most expensive pudding which was a banana split with fruit salad and masses of cream. I've forgotten the name of it.

It was now about 11 pm, and very impressed with my first ever restaurant meal, I paid the bill and walked out with a lollipop. It was a cold though dry November night as I walked along Lime Street towards the station. I had no idea what to expect. I was just living in the moment and loving every minute of it. I came to a brightly lit entrance of a large building from where a loud booming bass noise was coming from inside. It was called the Hippodrome. Curious, I walked straight in, paid a few pounds at the door and made my way to a bar. I got myself a cola and looked around. I was in a night club for the first time. The club was dimly lit and there weren't many people there yet. I walked onto the circular dance floor to stand next to a large five-foot speaker. It felt like a pneumatic drill was attacking my body and my ears were starting to feel numb. I saw that there was a staircase so went up and sat on my own on a sofa. A few minutes later two girls came upstairs and after a few minutes, one of them approached me and introduced herself as Lucy. We tried to chat but had to shout in each other's ears such was the crescendo. She found out that I was driving, probably since I was drinking cola, and asked if she could come back to mine after dropping her friend off. Not realising what she had in mind I agreed. Glad to get away from the din, I left the club with a girl on each arm. Lucy's friend lived near Strawberry Field in Woolton, a few miles away, and after dropping her off we went back to my apartment. It wasn't long before I had lost my virginity. I saw Lucy a couple more times until we both realised it was just a fling that we had wanted.

OUT

Within a few weeks of leaving home, I was to recruit an agent for the business I was running which was selling L'Arome perfumes. His name was Mark and he was about ten years older than me. Mark had been a lead singer of a band but he wanted to start a new one. When he found out that I played a twelve-string guitar he asked if I would join the new band he was putting together. It was to be called Tie Manic and the Manic Ties. Mark was manic. He was constantly tapping his foot and had a magnetic personality that made him friends wherever he went. He introduced me to the other members of his band, but we only ever practised a few times because we spent all our evenings in night clubs. Mark seemed to know all the night club owners in Liverpool and for the month I knew him, we went to about three clubs every night till the early hours. A few that I remember were The Continental Club, Pickwicks, The Grafton, The Montrose, and The She Club. We would usually end up in a dive in Wood Street or Fleet Street after hours. I drove everywhere as one pint was all I ever needed, and I am averse to hangovers. Mark's quest was to train me how to chat up women. I was clueless. My approach was when I saw an attractive lady I would immediately go right up and start chatting her up. This rarely worked and Mark kept telling me to play hard to get but his teaching never really worked.

Where were you on 25th February 1989? I went with Mark to a bar called The Coburg on Sefton Street to watch the long-awaited title fight between Frank Bruno and the then invincible Iron Mike Tyson on TV. The fight was in Las Vegas, so we didn't actually see it till the early hours of Sunday morning. The build-up was electrifying and we thought it was all over in the first round when Bruno was hammered to the floor. However, with about 50 seconds left in the round Tyson was caught with a left hook that staggered him for the first time in his professional career. He recovered and went on to knock Bruno out in the fifth round.

In keeping with his manic lifestyle, Mark won a Mini Metro in a Heinz competition. On his first day with it, the police found him driving it up the wrong side of the M56 motorway. They had him sectioned and that was the last I saw of him.

After a few months, my car came to the end of its life and therefore my business stopped. I signed on the dole which turned out to be for eight weeks. Being all by myself with no support I had to budget every penny. I was forced to take full responsibility or sink. I wrote a list of essentials and I remember my supper consisting of two pieces of toast, one with rationed cheese and the other with just margarine; Netto's finest.

I got a giro cheque every two weeks, I think it was about £54. One day, the day before my giro came, I had managed to save £3. Knowing I was getting paid the next day I went down to the local bookmakers on Lawrence Road and placed a £3 bet on Willie Carson doing the treble i.e. winning all three horse races. I then went home to watch the races on the TV. The horses shot out of the stalls and to my dismay Carson was coming last. As the race continued, he came through the field and won by a head. One down, two to go. The second race was exactly the same as the first. Carson coming last, advances through the field and wins. Surely, he won't do it again I thought. I had run a bath so taped the race so I could watch it after the bath. Race three. Carson coming last as usual, so I fast-forwarded the tape. As I did, he started to come through the field. I stopped the tape to watch it in real-time and Carson started dropping back. So, I fast-forwarded again and once again, Carson started overtaking the pack. Real-time again and Carson drops back. Fast forward again and was to see Carson storm through the field and win his hat-trick and my hat-trick! I won £70 and was able to have cheese on both slices of toast for supper.

During those eight weeks of not having a car, I would wander into town on foot which was about a thirty-minute walk. I would go down to the Pier Head at the River Mersey and watch the tide and the ferry boats crisscrossing the river. I loved the Pier Head with the seagulls, the salty air and the smell of doughnuts. I had fully accepted that this was my new life. I felt very alone but I liked the feeling. I have always been an extreme optimist and the unknown filled me with anticipation and excitement. After twenty-two years of suffocating rigid legalism and rules, my freedom felt priceless. I still had a very distant and scant feeling that the door to my parents and the EB was still there if I should ever change my mind enough. However, for now, I was relishing my freedom and the excitement and adventure of the unknown.

Walking down Huskisson Street just by the Liverpool Cathedral, I turned right into Hope Street and was met with a woman probably in her 40s. She looked a bit foreign, her hair was straggly, she wore baggy clothes, no front teeth and she looked ill. 'Do you want some business?' she asked me. Not knowing what she meant I said no and walked on. As I walked away it dawned on me that she might be a prostitute. I was so ignorant to the ways of the world. Curious I walked around the block to meet her again. She was still standing on the corner of Hope Street and so I asked her what business she was talking about. 'Ten for a gam or twenty-five inside' she said, 'I have a flat around the corner'. (To this day I'm not entirely sure what a gam is). I told her I had no money and walked on.

However, a seed was sown in my mind which was now racing with curiosity. I had taken a massive leap of faith in following my heart by leaving the EB, but I was vulnerable, and looking back I realise that I was not fully loving myself. I am not surprised at why I let my curiosity take me places. I had been so bored during the previous four years and like a bonsai tree that suddenly finds its roots are free to grow, I launched out naively with abandon.

At this point, I want to make it clear that the prostitutes I hired over the next two years was not a mature or healthy thing to do. I became addicted to the excitement, which like many addictions took over my life, and seemingly my free will too. I find it difficult to put in words but after every prostitute came a deep feeling of desolation, loneliness and regret. It was like my soul was drained every time. There were significant reasons why I went down this path. I recognise now that I had a deep wound and feeling of sorrow that my parents and everyone in my past had abandoned me, not directly, but because the rules they chose to obey amounted to just that. This feeling was also an internal anger and my addiction was a way of self-harming myself. This made me feel I was getting my own back on the cards that life had dealt me. I also had a very curious personality and a fascination in what people are thinking. Maybe I inherited some of this from the hours of sitting still in the EB meetings looking at the faces with not a lot more to do. To me, a person's mind was like a universe waiting to be explored. I also recognise that I didn't feel loved and though my parents did love me, their love was very much diluted and restrained by the lifestyle we lived.

As John Lennon wrote, All You Need is Love; he could not have spoken a truer word. I have learnt since that everything roots back to either unconditional love or a lack thereof. Where there is a lack there becomes a hole that requires being filled. I believe that every behaviour of mankind can be understood from this simple fact. In those two years of temporary pleasure I was not loving myself, but I was on a journey and I still am.

OUT

Does lightning ever strike twice? Near the end of my eight weeks on the dole, I find myself putting my last £3, this time on two dogs. I am in Lime Street at the bookmakers; Ladbrokes. My two greyhounds come in first and second and I walk out with £120. By the way, in my opinion, gambling is not mature or healthy either. Being just around the corner from Lime Street station, I went straight to the ticket office and bought a ticket to London Euston. Within a few hours, I was walking into the balmy evening air in the capital and made my way along Euston Road to find a cheap hotel for two nights. I had a plan. Growing up we used to play lots of board games. One of them was called London Cabbie. On a map of the main roads of the centre of London, you would drive around picking up and dropping off passengers. I had played this game so much that I could remember every street on the map. I was going to go on a walk that night to see if I could navigate my way around this real city without a map. After finding a back-street hotel costing £40 for two nights, I let myself into the small bedroom, hid most of my money under the bedsheets, and set off for my midnight walk. It fascinated me that I knew what street or road or monument was coming up next. I felt like Dick Whittington in control and on the verge of opportunity. It came alright .... in Soho. Pink and red neon lights lit up entrances everywhere. Ladies of the night stood outside encouraging people to come inside into their sex shows or peep shows. There were lots of flashing signs saying '£2 Live Sex Show.'

My curiosity inevitably got the better of me. I realised that these were not safe places to be on your own but £2 sounded reasonable to me so I entered through a beaded curtain to see a scantily dressed girl at a desk. She asked me for the £2 then handed me a drinks menu. I declined until she said that I couldn't see the show unless I had bought a drink. The cheapest drink was wine for £8 a glass. I ordered the wine. The girl told me to go down the stairs and take a seat and she'd be down with the drink. I climbed down rickety wooden stairs into a musty dimly lit basement room with a double bed in the middle. Around two of the walls were seats partitioned off with curtains so you could only see the bed and not who else was watching. After a few minutes, the girl came down with the wine which tasted like vinegar. She told me the show would begin soon and went back upstairs. I waited a long five minutes on my own. Then I heard voices and two men came down the stairs. They had come to see the show too and I could see that they were tough-looking with Cockney accents. They sat in the cubicle next to me a curtain separating us. The girl came down with the drinks and I heard an argument start. The girl was demanding something like £40 for the drinks and the men were saying that they were being ripped off. Suddenly the girl shouted out, 'Charlie come, there's trouble here.' Immediately the two men got up and ran up the stairs with me right behind them. I didn't want to meet Charlie whoever he was and wasn't going to risk additional charges being added to get to see the show.

In the first five or six months of leaving home, I ran up a phone bill for £3500. I couldn't pay it, got cut off, changed my number and ran up another bill for £800 before that was cut off too. How can someone without any friends run up such a bill? Chat lines. You simply had to call a premium rate phone number and speak to a woman about anything you like. I spent hours talking to women at night time. If I wasn't watching something on the TV, I was on the chat lines. These were advertised in tabloids and some of them cost £1 a minute. In time I learnt a lot about the chat line culture and how the women were never allowed to give away their location and certainly not meet anyone they chatted to. Primarily our conversations were about sex. I wanted to explore the mind of a woman and my curiosity drove me to many hundreds of hours of doing just that. I would get to find out who was online and at what time and have regular sessions with them as well as getting to know about them. It fascinated me to see how much information I could get them to divulge and my quest was to meet some of them. Bear in mind, when you are only chatting on a phone, you have no idea what the person you are speaking to looks like. They give descriptions but often they would exaggerate.

I can remember meeting two, both blind dates. The first one was from a Liverpool chat line. She was petite and cute, and we saw each other for a few weeks until I realised, she had lots of boyfriends.

The second one worked on a chat line in Seacombe, Wirral. Karen. I had chatted to her for weeks using every trick in the proverbial book to get her to divulge where she was and why we should meet. One night, maybe she had been drinking, she agreed to meet. I drove over to a lay-by on Birkenhead road, about 1 o'clock in the morning, near the Seacombe Ferry terminal. Along came Karen and got into my car. She was not the tall blonde, shapely, feminine model that I had imagined. Well, she was blonde. She was about fifteen years older than me and about fifteen stone too. I recognised her voice and we got on like a house on fire. Over the next few weeks, we became great friends. She lived in a terraced house in Seacombe just around the corner from her local pub called the Beehive. She was one of these 'salt of the earth' women with a loud cackle, a drinker of many pints and a heart of gold. Her son James lived with her and we became friends too.

It was around this time that I got held a hostage by a gang of drug dealers. Here is what happened.

I had been at a house in Huyton in Liverpool pitching a prospective agent to sell the perfumes for me. At the house was a friend of the client, Sharon, a woman in her 30s. She showed an interest in selling the perfume too and as I learnt that she was going over to the Wirral that day and because I was also going to Seacombe in Wirral, I offered her a lift. On the way I stopped at my house to go to the loo and collect some items and Sharon came in. When I finished, I went into my lounge noticing that the cupboard door was ajar where I stored some of my perfume stocks. I noticed some were missing and in the lounge by Sharon's feet was a plastic bag that looked full of perfume bottles.

What could I do? I was embarrassed. I decided to take one moment at a time so got back in the car with Sharon. Driving through the Mersey tunnel she pulled a knife out of her shoulder bag and demanded my cheque book and card. Funnily enough, I had deliberately left them in my bedroom as I had a gut feeling about Sharon. Shouting and swearing at me we exited the tunnel and she directed me to Green Lane where she said she wanted to be dropped off. I felt like I was in the movies in a thriller. I remained calm but was very scared inside. However, this was just the beginning. It was a Sunday and there was not much traffic about. I was looking for a police car to flag down. As I stopped the car at Green Lane by some waste ground, Sharon as quick as a flash, grabbed my car keys and jumped out of the car threatening to throw my keys down a grid and burn the car down. I jumped out of the car and caught her and tried to wrestle the keys off her. She was punching and scratching me and in trying to get the keys off her I wrestled her to the ground. Next thing she had put the keys down her knickers and started shouting out the names of people that she knew who lived in the flats nearby. Two youths ran out of the flats and we had a standoff. Sharon said if I wanted my keys back, I would have to give her and the two youths a lift. I had to make a decision instantly. I decided to go with the moment and agreed. The two youths got in the back of the car and Sharon in the front told me where to drive to. We drove to some council estate on the Wirral. Sharon got out and told the youths to keep an eye on me as she wanted to go somewhere after this call. One of the youths got a knife out and told me to wait for Sharon. Eventually, Sharon got back in the car and for the next four hours, she got me driving round the Wirral on a drug run, collecting and delivering drugs. There were no police cars out that afternoon unfortunately for me. The youths were under her control and at some point, asked me how I knew Sharon. I told them and they said I should have kept well away from her as she is a very dangerous drug dealer.

After four hours we had stopped outside a bungalow somewhere in Tranmere. Sharon went inside and a few minutes later a wild-looking man came out of the front door and pointing to me I heard him shout, 'Is that him?' I was gripped with fear assuming that Sharon had told him about our fight. Suddenly one of the youths said, 'Drive off mate, he's a psycho.' I sped off and the youths told me to drop them off back at Green Lane with the advice, 'Keep away from her.'

Feeling very relieved and shaken I drove straight to Karen's in Seacombe and told her the whole story. Karen was very streetwise and said that it was dangerous to return to my apartment as Sharon knew where I lived and might go there looking for me. She said I could stay at hers until things had died down. Fearing what she said could be true I immediately drove back to my apartment. I stuffed my car with all valuables including my TV and clothes and went to stay with Karen and her son James in Seacombe. I was to stay there for three months. It was the long hot summer of '89 and I have memories of many an idyllic day on the beach at New Brighton or Newbo as we called it. I remember watching The Ashes with David Gower and Angus Fraser failing to beat the Aussies that year. Simply Red was in the charts with the melancholy If You Don't Know Me By Now as was Guns and Roses with Sweet Child O' Mine and Wind Beneath My Wings sung by Bette Midler.

It was a three-month holiday and pretty much every evening Karen and I would end up in the Beehive pub half a minute walk from her house. They were great nights of playing pool, drinking Black Russians and Creme de Menthe and all being entertained by Karen and her cackles. On two occasions I was to get drunk, two out of the four times I have ever been drunk. I am still looking for a good reason to justify those nauseous, head-spinning hangovers and have yet to find one. The first time, I had been mixing my drinks with a few Carlsberg Special brews, for the road. All I remember is staggering out of the pub and seeing the grass verge by the roadside. I thought how incredibly comfortable it looked so lay down and was woken an hour later when Karen found me. The second time I crawled under the pool table and woke a few hours later after the pub had shut. I woke to the sounds and bangs of Karen engaging in coital activities on the pool table above me. This was another sex show that I missed.

Enter another person in the chapter of my two wild years of excess, indulging and pleasure. Sandy. She was a friend of Karen's and used to call round a few times a week in the evenings. She was 28 years old, friendly, curly blonde hair, and like myself, came from Liverpool. I can't remember whether or not she worked with Karen on the chat lines or not. Anyway, one night she had missed the last bus home so I, being too kind, offered her a lift to save her getting a taxi. She lived in Leasowe near the Oyster Catcher pub. When we arrived, she invited me in but to her horror saw that her house had been burgled and various items had gone missing. She just stood there motionless, for about five minutes, as if in a trance. She was obviously in shock. I didn't know what to do. I don't remember calling the police and it was about 1 o'clock in the morning. I had an idea. It had been three months since the saga with the drug dealer. Since then there was no evidence that my apartment had been visited and I wanted to move back. So, I decided to take Sandy back there overnight and hopefully, she would be alright in the morning.

She ended up staying three months and almost landed us both in jail. Here's what happened. We became good friends. Our lifestyle of late nights, lots of TV and videos, many slices of pizza and McDonald's turned into one lazy convenient three months of slobbing out and just existing till our money ran out. After a month Sandy wanted us to get married. When I said no, and that I certainly wasn't ready for marriage at this stage of my life, she was very upset. Then she told me a fantastic story.

Her mother had an uncle who owned a diamond mine in Argentina. He had given a substantial amount of money to Sandy's mother who lived in Liverpool. Also, Sandy had a brother who was married and who lived in Bootle Liverpool. When Sandy and her brother were to reach thirty-five years of age, half a million pounds, yes, £500,000 would be released to each of them. Her brother had just turned thirty-five and had received his lump sum and Sandy was twenty-eight. She told me that although her money wasn't for another seven years, she could ask her mum for an advance which she could pay back when she reached thirty-five. She said she was going to ask her for £50,000 from which we could start up a business as we were both out of work. We could also go on holiday and buy whatever we wanted. Imagine having that offered to you on a plate? I was very dubious about agreeing to this as I knew it would potentially tie me down to Sandy. However, the thought of financial freedom decided it for me.

Sandy arranged to see her mother that evening to ask her for the money and sort out the details.

I waited in my apartment and Sandy came back all smiles saying her Mum had agreed and tomorrow she would take her to the bank and arrange the transfer. Imagine that! We could hardly sleep with excitement and stayed up late making lists of all the things we were going to buy. The next afternoon Sandy went to arrange the transfer but returned an hour later saying that her Mum had said she was busy and instead to go at the end of the week. We were very disappointed but continued our list-making and spent that week researching and pricing the holiday, car, business and the many items we planned on buying. The big day arrived and Sandy went to her Mum's again only to return with her Mum giving her an excuse and saying come back on Monday to sort the money out. We were puzzled and very annoyed that such a life-changing happening could be postponed so easily. That weekend we carried on with our plans fully expecting third time lucky Monday would be jackpot day.

Monday came. Sandy went to her Mum's to return an hour later crying. I knew why. Her Mum had postponed it again. How could she do this to her daughter? How cruel to get someone's hopes up three times then dash them down with a feeble excuse. We were so angry and I suggested Sandy forget the whole thing. At that point, I only had her word for the whole story. I had not even met her Mum, but I believed Sandy was telling me the truth despite her desire to be married. However, was the whole story fabricated? Knowing how flimsy her story might have appeared to me Sandy said she was going to take me to see her Mum and get her, in front of me, to say what she was going to do about the £50,000. I agreed and that afternoon we went around to her Mum's house in Kensington Liverpool. Her Mum was out but Sandy had the front door key. The house was a small mid-terrace and looked rather run down. Inside was no better and a strong odour of cat wee greeted us. Sandy went upstairs telling me to wait downstairs in case her Mum came in. A few minutes later Sandy came down to show me three bank statements from different bank accounts in her Mum's name. My eyes opened wide when I saw that each one had more than a £100,000 balance.

A few minutes later Mrs Day arrived. She was probably in her late 50's though she looked a lot older with her curly white hair. She was very small, shabbily dressed in an old long coat and she carried a plastic carrier bag. She certainly didn't look like someone who had six figures in her bank account. Over a coffee the conversation went something like this:

Sandy: Mum, this is John my friend who I told you about. We want to go into business together.

Mrs Day (Sandy's mum): Hello John, nice to meet you.

Me: Hello Mrs Day, nice to meet you too.

Sandy: So, Mum, are you still ok with giving me the £50,000 advance?

Mrs Day: Yes, I will but I need a favour. On Sunday can John hire a car and drive me to Sheffield to my husband's grave, then to Denbigh in Wales to see a friend? I'll give you the cash now for the car. Then drop me back at mine Sunday night and pick me up in the morning at 9 o'clock. We will go to the bank and I will draw out £2000 cash and bankers order for £48,000.

Well, the jackpot was still on! I had heard it from the horse's mouth. It was a long wait to the weekend. On the Sunday morning, I went down to Avis Car Rental in Mount Pleasant with Sandy and hired an automatic Rover 820. It was a great car to drive. That day, I drove Mrs Day and Sandy to Sheffield and the grave, had roast beef and Yorkshire pudding in a pub en route, then drove the hundred or so miles to Denbigh in North Wales to see a friend of hers. We arrived back in Liverpool at midnight and had an early night in preparation for the long-awaited following day. That Monday morning's alarm clock was so welcome I can tell you. We were outside Mrs Day's house on the dot of 9 am. Sandy went in to collect her Mum. I waited 3 minutes, then 5, then 10, then 15, then 20. Each minute my heart sunk deeper and a feeling of great frustration and anger built up. After 20 minutes Sandy emerged and got in the car absolutely distraught. I remember shouting, 'Don't tell me, I don't want to know, I don't want to hear another lie from your Mum. She is a heartless F, B, T, C etc etc...' I drove the car back to Avis. Sandy later told me that her Mum had said that it wasn't a good time and to come back in a week.

That roller coaster disaster had been so emotionally draining. However, this wasn't the end of the story. Sandy had plan B which was to ask her brother for an advance. She asked him and he said no. Plan C. Sandy told me that when her dad had died when she was very young, he had left £5000 in a National Savings interest account. She felt so sorry for the saga and the stress that her Mum had caused me that she wanted to draw out the money and give it to me. I point blank refused. I could not take any money that her deceased father had left her. No way. Plan D. She would find out the interest that the account had accrued, give it to me and leave the original £5000 in the account. Foolishly I agreed. So, Sandy went to the Post Office and applied for the balance. A few days later she received a letter from them. The news was rather pleasing. The account had swelled to over £55,000! She had an application form to make a withdrawal. She wrote my name on to receive a cheque for the sum of £50,000. I went to a red pillar box with her and posted it and heard the letter fall to the bottom. The jackpot was on again.

So here we were again, £50,000 on the way. Out come the lists again. What could possibly go wrong now? A letter arrived about a week later from National Savings. There was a clause in the account that required the signature of none other than Mrs Day. Off goes Sandy to get her Mum's signature. As expected, she returns in tears as her Mum had said she was busy, come back in a week. Plan E. Sandy said she was going to forge her Mum's signature. She went to her mum's when she was out and found letters with her Mum's signature on. Then she practised copying them and signed the form to release the money. She would never find out she told me. The 50,000 was alive again!

That afternoon I called to see someone who had left the EB years before I did. Arnold Westwood. He had been a banker and accountant. I trusted him and told him the whole story from beginning to end. When I had finished, he said, 'Tell Sandy to get on the phone and cancel that request form immediately. With such a large sum of money, the bank will send a representative round to see Mrs Day to verify her signature. Sandy will end up in prison and you might be involved too. What a shock! I went straight back to Sandy and told her what Arnold had told me. She called National Savings and successfully cancelled the request. End of story. A week later Sandy moved out and I never saw her again. There were no hard feelings, but life had to move on. In ten years' time, I would have been 33!

Maybe there was a lesson to be learnt here. Don't chase money!

The last story about Sandy was that a week before she left, she found an advert in a local paper for a telesales representative and encouraged me to apply for the post. I applied and got the job which leads to the next episode in the two wild years after I left the EB.

The job was with a company called Autosearch, based in the

OUT

Brunswick Dock in Liverpool where car sellers were matched to car buyers. A team of telesales reps would call up people who were advertising their car for sale. We would tell them we could find a buyer for them and if they agreed we would take the details, and their money, which was about £40 to £60 depending on the car. I worked for Autosearch for 17 months with a team of 70 reps. Numbers and statistics were a fascination with me, maybe formed through all my counting and recording stats during the EB meetings. Competing in a group of 70 reps inspired me and during my time there I broke lots of records.

I loved our office life. There was always a buzz and lots of laughs. One time, Donna who was 18 stone, was sitting at work on one of those ridiculously thin spindly-legged plastic chairs. Suddenly she screamed. We all looked and saw her, unable to do anything, as the chair's back legs slowly collapsed, and she ended up flat on her back with her legs akimbo.

After about six months I was to experience a lesson that taught me what is still a constant quest of mine to this day; to live from my heart, not just from my head. I believe that true genius lies in the heart of everyone. Here is what happened. I experienced mental burn out. I could not lift the telephone to make a call. My head was so full of scripts and I found that I simply could not make another sales call. I cannot really explain it. I had a mental blockage somehow. I stared miserably at the phone for a couple of hours thinking that I would have to get another job. I felt immense frustration. Something was building up inside me like a pressure cooker.

Then it burst. A feeling of relief and peace mixed with utter 'I do not care anymore' washed through me. I knew exactly what I was going to do. I was not going to sell, coerce, manipulate, twist, embellish or exaggerate any more. As I said, I was not going to sell, I was now going to tell, tell the raw truth with vulnerable honesty and I cared not if everyone said no. I picked up the phone, dialled up a car seller, and with total nonchalance in a 'matter of fact' tone I spontaneously and slowly said the following:

Me: Hello, is the car still for sale please?

Car seller: Yes, it is.

Me: My name is John from Autosearch. We are the largest most successful car specialists for the UK, and I was just wondering if you would like us to register your car today and match you up to a buyer. (The last word 'buyer' was not in a high tone of a question but was in a lower tone of a statement)

Me still: SILENCE.

This silence was the product of raw honesty and total lack of 'selling.' It was genius. It was raw honesty speaking by using silence. Why? Because I was now not trying to make anyone buy. I wasn't going to try to push, sell or coerce. This silence showed that I believed in myself. The silence gave the seller space, respect and was devoid of sales pressure. For all I cared the seller could say no, but the silence spoke loud and clear. I got the sale, five sales that hour. The next week a competition started. The top rep each week out of the 70 would get a prize plus a £50 bonus. The prizes included weekend breaks and the use of the Director's red Lotus Esprit Turbo. With my 'given up, 'not trying,' not caring' new attitude and pitch, I got the most sales for the next five consecutive weeks. Since only I was getting the prizes, they stopped them after five weeks because it stopped being an incentive to the others.

I reckon that my EB upbringing forged a 'head' as opposed to a 'heart' existence in me. Logical, polarized, Bible-interpretation-based, chained to the bar of self-righteousness and boxed into the Leader's exacting laws, there was no room for the spontaneous, creative, exploratory, freedom of thought and expression. The former, I have come to see and experience, is not being true to oneself. The latter is to discover honesty and truth and ultimately means to love oneself, essential before we can love another.

Back to the story. Not long after the competition, in which I found my heart's expression, they promoted me to manager and gave me a company car to keep. Unlike the Director's car, it was a blue 1973 Mercedes 240D. It was so long that when you turned the large steering wheel, the Mercedes bonnet ornament seemed to move like the bow of a ship. I think it had done over 200,000 miles, it sounded like a tank, cost £300, used 5 litres of oil a week and the engine blew after three months. Still, no regrets, I scrapped it and got £150 for it.

My job as a manager was to get the sales of the company up to 1000 per week. Up to now, the record was about 600 a week. There were two other managers, Mary and Peter. Mary was a great down to earth Scouser from Kirby, about ten years older than me. Peter was 18, full of confidence and wore the best ties in the office. We were put on bonuses if we got the sales figures up, so the challenge was on. I got together with Mary and Peter and hatched a plan. We would tell the 70 reps that the company would be closing down if the sales figures didn't rise. We would be creating a chart each week showing the sales figures of each rep in a league table. If you were in the bottom ten for two weeks running, we would have no choice and unfortunately, you would have to leave.

This system caused great focus for all the reps. After two weeks and from thereon after, up to ten reps were skimmed off to be replaced with new reps. This process meant that the sales figures of the bottom ten were always rising causing an upward trend. Mary and I had a quiet word with Peter. We told him that we all have our strengths and that Peter's was definitely the ability to give the news to the reps who had to leave. Peter believed us and relished this opportunity to wield some power. It meant that Mary and I kept popular with everyone. After three months we reached 1000 sales.

I made lots of friends at my time in Autosearch. There was a close group of five of us that spent most of the time laughing when we were together. We had to sit apart in the office or else we would just set each other off laughing and get no work done. Ian was the master of mirth. His humour was dryer than dry and his straight faced-ness and ability to craft words with multiple meanings and inference was hilarious. Martin, also with drier than dry humour, kept us all laughing with his subtle wit, melancholia and intelligence. Tony was just an engine of zany comedy and seriousness at the same time. Then there was Kevin. When he joined us, he appeared to only have a serious side. After a few weeks with us, the comedian was released in him and he became a maverick of hilarity and the creator of some of our office's best wind-ups.

When you are spending lots of hours on the phone you need a break, something to refresh your mind and recharge your batteries. When a prospective customer would swear or be really nasty to any of us, we would make a note of his phone number. He then would be a candidate for a little challenging in the form of a wind-up. These wind-ups were not exactly ethical, but they were great fun. We would also record the conversations, as playing them back produced as much fun as actually doing them. Kevin seemed to have endless ideas and the best ever wind-ups came from his genius. 141 was dialled before the number so our number couldn't be traced. Here is one of them:

Rep 1: Hello is that Mr McGregor?

Mr M: Yes, speaking.

Rep 1: It's Jimmy here. When Dave phones up can you tell him that Jimmy says that the TV is fixed now. Thank you.

OUT

Mr M: I think you have the wrong number?

Rep 1. Is your number (reads out Mr M's number) and are you Mr Mcgregor?

Mr M: Yes, but...

Rep 1: In that case just pass the message on when Dave phones, thank you. (Slams the phone down.)

20 minutes later Rep 2 phones up:

Rep 2: Hello is that Mr McGregor?

Mr M: Yes, speaking.

Rep 2: When Dave calls, could you pass the message on that Ian says it's a definite no? Thanks

Mr M: Who is this calling?

Rep 2: It's Ian, and your number is (reads out Mr M's number) isn't it.

Mr M: Yes but...

Rep 2: Just tell Dave the answer is no. Thank you. (slams the phone down)

20 minutes later Rep 3 phones up:

Rep 3: Hello is that Mr McGregor?

Mr M: (Suspicious now) Who is this calling?

Rep 3: It's Paul, when Dave calls could you pass the message on that Paul says he's got the job. Thanks.

Mr M: (Getting angry) Now wait a minute, who are you?

Rep 3: I've told you, Paul, just pass the message on, I'm busy, bye. (Slams the phone down).

20 minutes later Rep 4 phones up:

Rep 4: Hello, any messages?

Mr M: Who are you?

Rep 4: I'm Dave, any messages for me?

Mr M: (Very angry) Who do you think you are?

Rep 4: I'm Dave just collecting my messages, you are Mr McGregor aren't you? Any messages?

Mr M: (Furious) &!@F&B@T^B etc...

Rep 4: Stop being such a nuisance, I'm just using your number as a message service for the next week or so. Any messages?

Mr M: Slams the phone down.

The moral of the story is be nice to sales reps on the phone,

OUT

Then there was the secretary, Sally. She was great fun, blonde, slim, early twenties, always lasted till the end on our Friday nights out, and always had a bad hangover on Saturdays. She always had a boyfriend, which meant that we were only ever just friends. Sally was always up for a laugh so when I asked her to manage my blind dates she happily agreed. I had noticed a Lonely Hearts section in the local free paper, the Merseymart. Using the office phone, I would phone up all the viable sounding ladies, and leave a message with the office number, asking them to phone my secretary who would arrange a date. One by one they called and sure enough, Sally fixed me up with five dates that coming week, all in the Moat House Hotel in Paradise Street.

I found that meeting strangers a most intriguing game. It wasn't just a game, it was basically a great way to spend a couple of hours with a nice person, getting to know each other. You never knew what you would learn, where it could lead to, what she would look like and if you would end up in bed or getting married or not. Well, you usually knew that within a few seconds. Gotta be in it to win it so they say. The most fascinating thing on earth for me is people's minds. I'd rather have a chat with a stranger than go to the zoo. I do love animals, but the mind of a person is intriguing with its unique labyrinth of permutations of thoughts, beliefs and experiences. So, if wedding bells was clearly not going to be happening, plenty more pleasure would be gained anyway. Some of the most interesting ladies I met were, how can I put it, not even a Picasso if a large poll was taken. Looks were not a deal-breaker. I was able to practice communication, discernment, and get to know a bit about another human in a couple of hours.

The Moat House hotel bar was waitress service. After the fourth night, after seeing me with four different women each night that week, the waitresses started giving me knowing smiles. Surely, they didn't think I was a gigolo, did they? After three weeks, they must have thought I was a very rich man. In those three weeks of blind dates, that Sally kindly arranged for me, I can only remember one lady. She was as attractive as, well, I'd rather not say, but she had been to all the Liverpool FC matches in the last ten years, home and away plus all the cup games and finals. We had a wonderful time, just chatting.

The Autosearch community had a great social life too. Every Friday evening about 20 of us would go into town. We would often start off at Trials Bar on Derby Square, a classy bar frequented with law firms and banking clientele, and us. Then we'd wander down Harrington Street to the less classy Pen and Wig, then via a few more bars including the Cavern Pub in Mathew Street, to the basement of The She Club on Victoria Street. I've no idea why we would often end up here, but I suspect it was because of its reputation of the women who went there for two reasons. One of them was to look pretty!

The club was dark and hot and was downstairs in a basement and was always packed like sardines. It was 1990 and us men from the office wore suits and competed with each other with who could wear the most outrageous tie.

We would spend most of the night on the dance floor break dancing till the last song; the infamous slowy. I loved moving my body to the music of the 90s. Techno was coming in with some incredible dance songs with my favourites being from Corona with her Baby Baby, Rhythm of The Night and Try Me Out. Then there was MC Sar and The Real McCoy with Runaway and Another Night and my all-time favourite Clock with Everybody. We danced so hard for so long that sometimes I would almost be sick. The last song was traditionally a slowy so-called because it was a slow song believe it or not. This would be the chance to 'cop off,'or 'bag off,' or 'get off,' or 'pull.' with one of the girls whose eye you had caught during the night. This meant dancing the slow song with her, holding each other tightly, usually snogging and a combination of either exchanging phone numbers, going home with her, going out with her, having a one-night stand with her or getting married. This last one, though rare, happened to one of our colleagues. I went to the wedding.

At 2 pm the bouncers and staff would start their mantras of, 'Drink up now please, could you finish your drink now, could you move towards the door please.' Our ritual was to go for a Chinese banquet. With about 12 of us left, we would make our way to up to the top of Duke Street and see if we could get a table in Chinatown. I always drove as I valued the ability to go anywhere anytime.

I valued this more than waiting in a freezing queue for an hour for a taxi with a hangover for a bonus on Saturday morning. Therefore, I was always sober with the rest staggering behind me. This meant that I could decide where we were going with little resistance. We would usually end up at Yams or Wongs where the chicken sweet corn soup, sweet and sour chicken and crispy duck with hoisin sauce always made you want to go back for more.

OUT

In this era in the late 80s, town was heaving every weekend and most of the night-lifers appeared to down as many pints or shorts as they could before the official closing time at 2 pm. There were always fights and brawling going on. Fortunately, I happened to have a good eye for it and managed to never get involved. My aversion to trouble and violence meant I always avoided eye contact with such aggressive gentlemen and I probably gave off a vibe of innocence. I saw many extremes that I was shielded from in the EB. I experienced the joy of dancing to great music, having wonderful times with lots of great friends, many late-night Chinese banquets, seeing violent street fights, blood, ripped clothing, steaming vomit on pavements and dance floors, half-naked women, three quarter naked women, people in all different shapes, sizes, and humanity up close and personal. It was not all 'mature and healthy' but at least I was moving. A ship can't turn around when it is stuck in the dock.

So, as I write this, looking back over those two wild years after leaving the EB, I reflect on all that happened and ask myself, 'What was that all about?'

Maybe I had been like a dodgem car at the fairground, going around in circles, and coming to terms with moving obstacles instead of the fixed rigid obstructions of my old lifestyle. I certainly enjoyed the ride. Maybe my increasing realisation of the unspeakable value of freedom, meant it was inevitable that I would eventually strike out; for gold. What gave me the resolve to make that gargantuan break from the traditions of my Fathers? Why did I not slump into depression, anger and bitterness?

What I saw on my 22nd birthday was so clear, so profoundly obvious, so motivating, that in a moment I had made a total single-minded commitment.

"In ten years from today, I am going to be 32. I am not going to spend another ten years being unhappy. I am going into the world 100% and if I ever get my head round to come back to the Exclusive Brethren then I shall, but, only if I can do it 100%. Sorry Lord, I tried to please you, but I've failed."

A wise man once said that 'a double-minded man is unstable in all his ways.' I found this to be absolutely true. My absolute commitment gave me the stability to sustain my escape until the time came when

OUT

eventually I could understand that this break from my past was one of the best decisions of my life.

   Perhaps, by the end of this book, you will agree with me.

Chapter 11

Freedom from Indoctrination

the epiphany

I wept uncontrollably as the realisation struck me deep in my heart. I saw with crystal clarity for the first time that it was a religious cult that I had been born into. I had lived a life deceived by men, who I could now see were trapped in a vortex of indoctrination and whose leader changed his rules whenever he wanted to. My parents, also born into it were still fully immersed in it. I could now see clearly that going back was impossible. How could I ever go back to what I now could see was a man-made fake? I couldn't, and it hit me hard that unless my parents who I love ever came out, I might never see them again.

This all happened in the early hours of Sunday morning on 23rd December 1990. A nine-hour conversation with my older brother Andrew was coming to an end. I would leave his apartment and go home a different person, a different aim in life, different values and a completely new perspective to explore.

Let me take you back a few months earlier that year when I had met my brother for the first time in nine years. I had not seen him since he left home and walked out of the EB just after his 16th birthday. I wanted to see him. He was my brother. The EB had shut him up (suspended him from attending any meetings) at the age of 15 and he spent his last few weeks until he turned 16, barricaded in his bedroom. When the 'priests' came around every Monday night to interrogate him, he refused to come downstairs to see them, so they would stand outside his bedroom door trying to talk to him through the closed door. From my bedroom, I could hear their rhetoric as they tried to persuade this 15-year-old school child to conform to the way of thinking of their Man of God.

This man had never met my brother Andy, yet he thought his interpretation of the Bible warranted two of his followers insisting on the enforcement of his law through the closed bedroom door. Looking back, I remember thinking how awkward and humiliating all this was for my brother, who in effect was just a minor, having to put up with that potentially psychologically damaging and bigoted religious behaviour. Andy had been 'shut up' for going to a school friend's house after school and for listening to Elvis, Eddie Cochrane, Gene Vincent and that era of music. I remember him describing to me how incredible their guitar playing was. At the age of 16, when it was legal for him to leave home without parental consent, he walked out, and I didn't see him again for nine years.

As soon as I left home on that Monday morning, 7th November 1988, I started searching for Andy. I went to libraries to look up electoral roles, tried to contact his old school acquaintances and even visited random night clubs that played rockabilly music and where I thought he might have gone. I didn't find him. Then one day late in the autumn of 1990 I came home to my apartment to find a note had been put through my door. It read:

Hi, I am your brother Andy give me a ring on (phone number).

I called the number and was surprised to hear a strong Scouse North Liverpool accent. We had been brought up in South Liverpool where the accent is softer. We arranged to meet the next day. I drove the 7 miles to his apartment in Crosby, North Liverpool and rang the doorbell. I didn't know what to expect. A 6-foot 2 man wearing an army jacket and jeans, short hair back and sides, wearing rimless glasses opened the door to me and shook my hand. "Alright John, I'm Andy, how are you doing?"

He told me that he was given my address by our Aunt Julia who lived in New Zealand. She, and her husband, Uncle Alan Spinks, and our six cousins had left the EB in 1970 after the Aberdeen split. They had emigrated there and that was the end of them as far as we were concerned. Somehow, on a grapevine maybe, my Aunt had heard that I had left the EB. She had found Andy's address via the Salvation Army, who hold information on millions of people, and had written to Andy to tell him that I had left and to get in touch with me to see how I was.

OUT

Andy told me that after leaving the EB, he had blocked out all memory of his childhood and didn't instantly realise who this John Spinks was for a few days. Then he remembered and went and posted the note through my door.

For a couple of months, we met regularly and spoke a lot about cars, business and money-making opportunities. We avoided the subject of our childhood and the EB. From Andy's side, he had blocked out the childhood EB memories and had even changed his surname by deed poll to distance himself from his past. From my side, upon leaving the EB two years previously, I had decided not to talk to anyone about God or religion. Three groups of people in those two years had approached me in the street wanting to talk about God and I had told them I wasn't interested. This was because I still believed that the EB way was the only way and it was a sheer waste of time talking to anyone with different views. I had in the back of my mind to eventually encourage Andy to go back to the EB if he was able to.

So that Saturday 22nd December, I went up to Crosby at 6 o'clock in the evening to see Andy again. It had been a bitterly cold day and the roads were just beginning to sparkle with ice crystals. Around the corner from where Andy lived in Crosby was a 'chippie' called the College Road Supper Bar, sadly not there anymore. They cooked the most incredible sweet and sour chicken and chips and Barbeque Spare Ribs. The chicken was always six large tender pieces of breast cooked in batter then marinated, in a silver foil tray, filled with loads of tangy sweet and sour sauce with pineapple and peppers. The pork ribs were large, tender and succulent dripping in a delicious sticky barbeque sauce. Am I making you hungry? We would often get our tea there and take it a mile away to Burbo Bank, a stretch of promenade which overlooks the River Mersey estuary and the Irish Sea. Sitting in the car this evening we tucked into our sweet and sour and the conversation changed.

Andy told me that he had been getting to know me over the past couple of months because there was something he wanted to tell me, and he hadn't been sure when the right time was. He said it was about the EB and God. I immediately gave my viewpoint of the EB infallible doctrines and how that they were the way, the truth and the life. Andy listened patiently then replied and our conversation was to continue on till 3 am, by which time we had gone back to his apartment.

Here is something rather significant. I was completely closed off to talking about God as I deemed it a sheer waste of time, but because

OUT

Andy was my brother, I listened to him. I reckon I would not have listened to anyone else. I shall digress slightly with a story that happened earlier that year which appears linked to this significance.

In the summer of 1990, a few months before I met Andrew, I decided to visit two psychic-type people. I was curious and ignorant as to how potentially lethal, in my opinion, their influence and enchantings can be. The first was a tarot card reader in Manchester who, I, of course, had never met before. I walked into her space and the first thing she said was, 'Hello John.' I quickly looked at my sports bag to see if there was a label with my name on. There wasn't. If she had said any other name I would have walked out. I was enchanted so paid her fee and sat down. She did her tarot card shuffling, told me stuff about things that made no sense, then or since, but then she said the following. 'You have had a big family upset and near the end of the year you will be living with family in Australasia.'

A few days later I was to visit a palm reader in New Brighton. I went in his little tent and he had a look at my hand. All I do remember him saying was that later on this year, I would be living in Australasia. A few days later I received a letter from my Uncle Alan and Aunt Julia in New Zealand offering me a plane ticket and instructions to fly to their home at the end of October and live with them. Well, it was all adding up and seemed like 'fate' was happening. So, I followed the directions, went down to London to New Zealand House and got a visa stamped on my passport. Everything was slotting into place. I started sorting out my affairs which included settling my bills. It got to October and I had an electricity bill outstanding for about £60. It wasn't a lot but for some reason, a bit strange looking back, I wrote to my Uncle and Aunt and asked them if they could help me out with it. I received a letter back saying that they wouldn't. All of a sudden, it occurred to me that if they were unwilling to help me out with a small amount, what would it be like living with them 12,000 miles away? It was a one-way ticket. What was I letting myself in for? I had a strong gut feeling. Don't go. A few days before I was all set to fly, I wrote back thanking them for the thought of letting me live with them but that I was declining their offer. The next day, I was to get the note from Andy through my front door. At that time, and to this day, I believe I was meant to meet Andy. He was a vital key in the unlocking of my brainwashed entrapment and my freedom, for as I have already said, I would not have listened to anyone else. If I had followed the direction of the two psychics, I would have ended up the furthest place away from him on the planet!

OUT

So, back to the conversation. This is where you may find this story gets a bit weird, but I am just telling you what my brother told me. What happened next was the sequence of me getting free from the EB indoctrination.

Andy told me about meeting a man two years before in Spindles Health Club gym in Liverpool city centre, where he used to work out. Ken from Anfield had told him something about speaking in tongues whereby a person literally has the ability to speak in a language that he hasn't learnt. Andy thought he was talking about an Eastern religion and was very surprised when Ken showed him that there are about 27 references in the Bible to speaking in tongues and what it was.

Ken had told Andy that this still happened today and that literally millions of people experienced this miracle and its profound effects every day. On top of that, many people who believed in this also saw supernatural physical healings. I was very skeptical and had many questions, but the main ones were about what had Andy personally experienced and what the source of these alleged miracles were.

Andy told me that a few weeks after meeting Ken, his curiosity had led him to privately do what Ken had shown him about this speaking in tongues, which was to ask Jesus for his Holy Spirit. Upon doing this Andy had been shocked when he suddenly found he could speak fluently in a foreign language.

He described it like life-changing from black and white to full colour and from two dimensional to many dimensions. He said that whenever he spoke in tongues, love would rise up inside him as if it was coming to the forefront of his mind and it would change the way he saw and felt about people.

Although I was brought up to believe in the stories about the miracles Jesus did, I found it incredulous that in 1990 at the age of 24, no one had told me that miracles still happen today. In my 22 years in the EB, I had never heard of any miracles or the speaking of tongues that Jesus spoke about still happening today.

I wanted to know why these things didn't appear to be common knowledge.

Andy told me that many 'Christian' churches say that speaking in tongues has ceased which explains why they reject it. Most religions don't believe they have ever existed.

OUT

At this point, I want to tell you, the reader, that I am not trying to tell you to believe anything. I am just telling my experience. Back to the story...

So, I asked Andy why JN Darby and the subsequent EB 'Men of God', had not appeared to follow the Bible regarding speaking in tongues and the miracles for today. What Andy then said made one of the biggest impacts on my life that I have ever had. He told me that man changes but God doesn't and showed me the following from the book of Hebrews in the Bible:

"Jesus Christ the same yesterday, and today, and forever."

In that moment my life changed. You have heard about people saying they have seen the light, that epiphany moment where a revelation dawns and what was once darkness becomes illuminated with brilliant light. I couldn't stop crying. Here is what I saw and felt:

Man, with his puny attempts to control, had to keep changing his laws and regulations to maintain power. He has to enforce rules that get stricter and stricter. He changes the goalposts, increases the height of the bar, and adds more hoops to jump through, yet Jesus remains the same.

In that moment I realised that I had been indoctrinated and deceived. I saw with crystal clarity that I had been born into a religious cult and if my parents didn't leave the EB I might never see them again. My faint hope of one day getting my head back to being able to follow the EB rules again was smashed forever.

Chapter 12

The evolution of my beliefs from law to love

Why I am not religious, but I still love God

IF YOU HAPPEN TO WANT TO READ THIS CHAPTER, I'D LIKE TO FIRST SAY THAT THESE ARE MY JOURNEY'S MILESTONES AND I HAVE NO AGENDA TO WANT TO MAKE YOU BELIEVE WHAT I CLAIM TO HAVE SEEN AND EXPERIENCED. IT IS JUST PART OF MY STORY.

IF YOU'D RATHER NOT READ ABOUT ANY 'GOD' STUFF, I UNDERSTAND. INSTEAD, YOU MIGHT LIKE TO GO TO THE END OF THIS CHAPTER AND JUST READ THE LAST FIVE LINES OF THE POEM. THAT DESCRIBES MY 'RELIGION' NOWADAYS.

My belief about God during and after the Exclusive Brethren.

Over the years, I have noticed that when people leave their old religious cults, they seem to either give up on God totally and stop believing, put God on hold, or they go on a journey to discover more.

I sometimes get asked if my beliefs in God have changed since my Exclusive Brethren years. People ask if my experiences have put me off believing in God. I understand the curiosity and therefore I shall share the evolution of my beliefs but, although I'm not saying you would, and I'm sure you won't, don't just believe my beliefs. Question everything. Question questioning everything. Who says you can't?

At first glance, it appears that God is invisible and so perceptions about him tend to be what we see reflected in the people we look to, who we might believe represent God. Therefore, my first beliefs about God came from the EB behaviour and their beliefs which drove their actions. Most of the eleven meetings a week were about the Bible but only in the context of how the Man of God interpreted it. This coupled with the EB version of laws and rules formed in me a belief about what God was like.

God was, therefore, a remote God in heaven up beyond the skies. He required me to be good and to keep a 'clean sheet' daily. This meant 'repenting' of all the sins I committed each day. The Bible's Old Testament and New Testament appeared to be full of lists of sins which you could never totally avoid, so my life was very sin conscious. Repentance as I was taught meant confessing all your sins to God and turning away from them. This belief meant that God did not forgive my sins until I had confessed and stopped doing them. Repetitive sins meant you just hoped God had forgiven you. If I was having a few days or so where I thought I had hardly sinned, I would start to feel good about myself. With this attitude, pride would rise up and I would notice others who appeared to be sinning. I would judge them and look down on them and their 'wickedness'. Then as I started to fall into temptations myself, I would feel down about my lack of discipline and my performance. This would lead me to feel unworthy and distant from God who surely was frowning at me, I thought. Those who were judging me were certainly frowning at me as their self-righteousness was exposed to my 'uncleanness.'

Can you imagine thinking that this is your identity? Can you imagine how all this could screw a person up in their head?

And so, the cycle went on and on, and on. This religious maintenance programme certainly screwed me up. It was like being on a hamster wheel that never stops and you can never get off. God was used mostly as a confession tool. As I was taught, He could send people to eternal conscious torment forever and ever; He obviously had to be feared. The whole Bible was always interpreted in this context and the whole EB belief system was a set of laws and rules with a wrathful God to face if you dared disobey. After all, if God sanctioned the separation of husbands, wives and children with rules that over time were changeable, then he most certainly was a God to be scared of. This belief system was backed up, not with just a handful of references, but the use of countless Bible verses and all the ministry of the Men of God since JN Darby. The more you heard about it, which was every meeting, the more the EB 'message' was drummed into you from hundreds of angles, all fitting into place and agreed by everyone. Little did I know that thousands of cults all make the whole of their holy book fit their interpretations too.

Despite my EB beliefs...

When I was 12, I was in my bedroom on my own. It was here I believe God revealed himself to me.

Imagine being on your own in your bedroom. Suddenly an intense feeling comes over you of incredible overwhelming love like you have never come close to feeling before. This feeling of being loved so intensely touches your heart deeply and you are unable to contain yourself. You spontaneously burst into tears. Just as you know your mother's voice, you know this is Jesus and he is pouring his love into you. It feels like his love is filling you up until it overflows. From your heart, the overflow of love compels you to call out to him and with the intense love you feel, you tell him how much you love him and want him. You say, 'Jesus, I love you, I want you!' It is like standing in a brilliant light and all you know is his love. This is what happened to me.

After this experience, I came downstairs back into the EB lifestyle and law. The realisation of that first love was to stay with me deep in my heart and has never left me to this day. However, within a short time of coming back downstairs from my bedroom, my EB belief system took over like weeds choking a sapling. The feeling receded, taken over by conditions and laws but the memory never left me.

During the next ten years, I believed I could only get close to God by complying with the EB laws and rules and conforming to their lifestyle. Trying to keep the laws caused a yoyo existence of being religiously minded and judgemental whenever I thought I was being a 'good' boy, and despondency and feeling separate from God when I thought I was being a 'bad' boy. I would say that since 12, apart from that genuine love encounter, I mostly had a head knowledge relationship with God based largely on theory and EB doctrine about their version of God. This equated to a relationship with God that was dry, sterile and mediated through a man; the 'Man of God' that I was brought up to follow.

I gave up on trying to keep 'the laws.'

When I left the EB at the age of 22 I told God that I was taking a break. I had tried, but I couldn't keep what I thought were all his laws and demands that the EB expected off me. Therefore, I was going to go 100% into the 'world' and if I ever got my head back to following him

100%, I would do. During the next two years, I always felt deep down that God loved me which gave me a sense of peace. I recognise that this came from my experience when I was 12.

From the Frying Pan...

You know I've been telling you about how I escaped from the cult I was born into. Well, I was 22 when I eventually got out, but two years later, guess what? From the age of 24, I was to fall headlong back into a completely different religious cult, for almost six years. Here, I ended up fully immersed and indoctrinated into yet another set of teachings. How on earth could this have happened after the first experience? Quite easily in fact.

Two years after leaving the Exclusive Brethren, I met my older brother Andrew who I hadn't seen for nine years. During a nine-hour conversation one evening and into the next morning, he told me the story of his experience that had led him to a group of people that he was now a member of. With hindsight what he told me consisted of some amazing truths mixed with very subtle deception.

He gave me a seemingly watertight interpretation of the Bible regarding the subject of all people either saved to heaven or lost to hell for eternity. There are many such interpretations which through religion's distorted lens all appear watertight. However, the interpretation he gave me was also linked to supernatural signs and literal miracles that would happen if I actually did what he showed me the Bible says to do. I followed what the Bible says regarding the signs and miracles and amazingly they happened to me personally. This naturally appeared to authenticate the Bible interpretation that he gave me, and I was hooked. I had proof, not just a theory. The theories/teachings/ indoctrinations of this second cult were heavily taught in fine detail. The usual system of cultic control and fear was used to keep members following their way.

So, while I still relished my freedom, there was still a background fear of hell, eternal conscious torment, which was a value I still held from the first cult, and it was reactivated in the second cult. I really believed that would happen to me if I was not a conforming member.

This second religious group that my brother had been in for two years, was called Revival Centres International (RCI). From what I remember, there were only about 2000 members, mostly in Australia and the UK. The leader was Lloyd Longfield, a charismatic who, with his 'special revelation,' indoctrinated his followers with his heaven/hell theories keeping them in fear of breaking the laws and the rules he enforced.

RCI was very deep in its theology with many strands of doctrines that their pastors could weave into one unbreakable rope so to speak. Disobey these doctrines and eternal damnation would be your reward. As usual, the rules and laws that were in place were guarded by the 'oversight' (the RCI police) who could be like sergeant majors. There were bans on alcohol, smoking, 18 certificate films, visiting other churches, marrying outside their group and much more.

Seduced into going back under law again.

My belief in God had changed to now seeing him as a God of power, not just a dry self-righteous religion in a book. However, there was a mixture because Revival Centres was still another 'separation from evil' cult with their own version of what evil was. Therefore, I was very much under their particular rules and regulations, all of course, from their Bible interpretations which amounted to one word; Law. I was now back under law again, their law. There were conditions that required being met. This second cult was into heavy doctrine, going deep into the Hebrew and Greek text of the Bible. 'Truth' was worked out by counting words and debating their meanings. They searched the scriptures thinking that was the way to know God. Into the mix, they brought in theories and esoteric knowledge that affirmed to us that we knew more than most religions. They put the burdens of their laws on us all and expected us to carry these burdens. 'It's all in the Bible,' was their mantra, as it is for all Bible cults or 'holy book' cults. However, there was gold that we experienced too. There was the continual encouragement for all to speak in tongues each day which has the effect of strengthening, encouraging and comforting deep within. However, much of this encouragement was interpreted through the RCI filters. Then there was the faith to heal the sick which brought great joy and revealed that God is not just letters on a book, He still wants to flow his love and power through anyone who believes that it is still for today.

So, during those years, my belief about God was that he still required me to be under the cult's versions of law, 'proven' from their strict rigid Bible interpretation, and also that he manifests himself through his Spirit with signs and healings. I sure had a lot to learn. I still have.

RCI had a methodology to decide their beliefs using Hebrew, Greek and English meanings of words using dictionary definitions, counting occurrences of a word in the Bible, using a Strong's Concordance, dogmatic interpretations of their End Times and prophecy theories,

Bible Numerics, King James Bible version only and obscure theories of the Pyramids and British Israel. They had many teachings on other cults especially anti-Catholic teaching on Mystery Babylon religion and other esoteric knowledge which all neatly proved to them they were the 'true' church. They wove their private interpretations from Genesis to Revelation together and when you looked through the lens they look through, it all seemed to make sense. We were never told that there are over 40,000 denominations in the world that have their own seemingly watertight packages too, all believing that they are the 'right church/religion.'

During my time in the RCI, there was a split. Denominations split by default, as people, usually leaders, get new notions and new ideas. RCI split while I was there and we rebranded as 'Revival Fellowships.'(RF). I remember the division was over some hair-splitting policies including RCI banning bikinis on the beach. In Liverpool, we continued on the 'right' path (RF), leaving the 'compromised Pentecostals,' as we called them, to take their chances on 'eternal hellfire.'

However, a wonderful part of their belief and practice were miracles including healing of the sick literally. I witnessed this many times and though it was absolutely genuine, it was used to authenticate all the other stuff. That was why I made the mistake of going back into another cult. It was my first exposure to this side of Christianity, and it enchanted me into buying the whole package so to speak. Instead of just chewing the meat and spitting out the bones, I ate the whole cow!!

In relation to the evolution of my beliefs in God, I shall just mention here two of the things that I experienced and which much of Christendom says has ceased. Jesus said directly just before he died, that believers in him would speak in new tongues. Tongues are languages. He also taught his followers to heal the sick. I don't want this chapter to be a theological quoting of scriptures as I am not trying to prove anything to you. All I believed was that Jesus is the Son of God and whatever he said was the truth, whether I understood it or not. If Jesus said believers would speak in tongues and heal the sick, then, how could I? Jesus told us to ask for the Holy Spirit, so I did. I did not ask a book or a church, or a religion or a leader. Instead, I asked Jesus who I believed had risen from the dead and who is alive. As I asked him, I found myself speaking in a new language literally. I found myself speaking fluently and I can anytime I choose to. At first glance, this may sound foolish and improbable. What was amazing was that as I spoke in tongues, I was filled with incredible love for everyone. It was like cataracts had been removed from my eyes. I saw through eyes of love. Everyone was a unique, special, very precious and beautiful individual. I learnt that I had been filled with the Holy Spirit who is Love. The very thing that Jesus said would happen, about 2000 years ago, was happening to me. When you love people there is no place for separation, greed, control, weapons, war or hatred.

Miracles still happen today.

Then, with the awakening of the Holy Spirit came power. Not power to control people and gain notoriety or build an empire, but power to love and to heal the sick and much more. I saw miracles. I saw a short leg physically grow on my best friend's mother, hair appeared on a bald lady I knew, cervical cancer disappeared on another friend's mother, broken bones in the hand of my car mechanic were instantly made whole, a centimetre square hole in my car exhaust disappeared, drug and alcohol addicts lost their desire, hopeless people were filled with hope and joy and many more wonderful things. This was not the religion of talking about the label on a bottle. This was drinking the wine. Then I researched and found that many thousands of these things that Jesus said would happen, were happening all over the world today. I had been completely oblivious to all this because, listen to this...

In the EB, I had been locked in an enclosed group that did not believe that these things still happen today! They were completely oblivious and so was I.

Jesus said that these signs would follow believers, not non-believers. That made sense to me. (I am not saying that all EB members are non-believers. However, they didn't believe in the speaking in tongues and healing the sick that Jesus taught about. So, the signs, therefore, don't follow them, at the moment).

From the moment I first spoke in tongues, on 23rd December 1990, it was like God became full colour and ten-dimensional to me, instead of being mostly historic facts and figures and two dimensional. I began to realise that there was more to God than what I had previously been taught, much, much more.

So, all these supernatural happenings were used to substantiate that all our other Bible interpretations were correct and therefore they were the right group with the right leader to follow. They even boasted that if a member could ever disprove their doctrines, they would have to leave to be faithful to the group.

Well, my brother Andrew and I were more serious about these

doctrines than most. We lived under the constant fear of going to hell should we slip up. The Exclusive Brethren teaching had got us started on that one. Using the intellectual methodologies we were taught to interpret the Bible, we saw major discrepancies in the RF teachings. Eventually, we asked questions that could not be answered. We contacted all of the six UK RF pastors and called a local meeting to put the cards on the table. None of the pastors in the UK could show that our theories were wrong, and one even agreed with us. We walked out of that last meeting, into a sunny afternoon on September 28th, 1996 and never looked back. I do miss all my friends from there. They are all great people but are all banned from hanging out with people that they view as heretics like me.

Anyway, I cannot tell you the wonderful feeling of release and freedom as I walked away from the clutches of man's control and law, again. I did not realise the effect it had been having on me until I extracted myself from its tentacles. We had to leave to be 'faithful' to the remaining members who were now all 'compromised and left behind,' and would all be going to hell for believing false doctrine. Can you believe that this sort of nonsense goes on nowadays? It sure does.

However, although I was free from man's control, I wasn't quite out of the woods yet. I now had a new revised theology, even more watertight than before, which meant I was paralysed from mixing with other Christians. I would need another book to explain the complexities of all the theological issues but because they are all law-based junk, I won't waste your time. Anyway, I now had a problem. I could see other theories, that if true, would dissolve what I could see. I had to be true to myself. Heaven or hell was at stake here, or so I thought. I visited many places seeking answers. I made a chart with 'for and against' which changed each day. For four months I studied and researched these doctrines in a place of torment. I remember feeling that I would be trapped for the rest of my life in this vortex of confusion. Would I ever be able to sit down at peace with other people, who weren't like me?

After four months I was at the end of my tether. A good place to be. I called three friends who were still in RF but were on the edge of leaving. They still met with me secretly to avoid the wrath of the oversight. If they had been caught with me they would have been dis-fellowshipped with immediate effect. It was one of those type of cults. So, I met with friends, John, Jasper and Cathy in a flat in Walton, Liverpool. Our purpose was to pray in tongues until the answer to the doctrinal issues were revealed. I cannot describe how important this was to me. I'd liken it to feeling trapped on the moon with no way of getting back to earth.

Well, after an hour of praying in tongues, I suddenly got the answer! It came out of the blue and all of a sudden, I could see it and feel it and know it. My four months of torment dissolved. The answer that came wasn't the doctrinal answer to my questions. The answer was Jesus saying, 'hold my hand.' In that moment I could see that by trusting him and taking his hand I was safe. If we walked on a 3000-foot precipice I was safe. If we walked through the 'valley of the shadow of death' I was safe. No matter what dangers or enemies around me, I was safe. I didn't need to get 100% in a doctrinal exam anymore. By holding his hand, he would keep me and he was all I needed. Wow! It was as if the sun had come out and I was bathed instantly in light and peace. My heart was filled with joy. I told my friends but they didn't see it. They continued searching for answers. In this place of rest, I let go of my need and idol of knowledge. The false need of having to know all the answers and having to have a watertight package of doctrine was replaced. It was replaced with knowing how much I am loved!

Despite being under religious law…

Again, when I was 28, I was to be smitten by this love that was too powerful for my emotions. A few months before, I had prayed that I would see God's love again and that it would overcome the iron grip that I had always had on my emotions. I hardly ever cried as maybe my male English pride was so strong.

So, one evening, I was in a house in Norris Green, Liverpool. A group of us were in a circle in the lounge and I had a clear vision. Jesus was walking around the circle looking at everyone. When he came to me, he looked directly into my eyes. It was like I was suddenly consumed with love so ardent, so deep and kind, so intensely compassionate, so utterly for me, that I burst into tears in front of everyone. I ran upstairs to the loo where I physically could not stop weeping for half an hour. I tried to stop as I was so ridiculously embarrassed crying in front of my friends. After half an hour I managed to control myself and come downstairs. I so regret my trying to quench the effects of that vision but it sure broke that iron grip on my emotions.

Within a year of leaving that second cult, at the age of 30, I visited a church building one evening in Birkenhead. I was sitting on the front row at the end of the service. I suddenly found myself saying from my heart, 'Come to me Lord Jesus, come to me,' About seven foot in front of me I became aware of an invisible yet tangible presence. From this presence was flowing waves of unspeakably powerful love. As it touched me, I fell back into my seat and wept uncontrollably for 20 minutes as the intense love immersed me. I was helpless. It was like this love disarmed me of all need to perform or conform. I was being unconditionally loved and accepted just as I was, right there and then.

The paradigm shift.

A significant shift happened when I was 31. Without going through the long story, I came to glimpse the value in everyone. Although the Exclusive Brethren allowed any male to speak in their reading meetings, the 'church' tradition that I had experienced since then had been the clergy/laity model. This is where you have professional Ministers who do the talking in a church service, and the laity who generally are passive spectators in a congregation. They 'go to church' on a Sunday to hear the titled Minister or Pastor or Vicar etc who in effect is a 'one-man ministry.' The brief history of this is that Constantine, in around 300AD decided to make 'church' the state religion. He erected large buildings, then hired professional clergymen to take over. 'Church,' that had been persecuted believers, all ministering to each other, meeting in caves and houses, became an organised state religion. This same model is so 'normal' nowadays that it is taken for granted that you are either an active minister/clergyman or a passive spectator layperson.

My glimpse of the value in everyone happened by accident when I started going to a house group across the field from where I lived in Stoneby Drive, New Brighton. Long story short, the 'Pastor' went away for 12 weeks so we were left without a man to lead us. Instead, we all decided to ask the Holy Spirit to lead us. What happened in those next 12 weeks 'blew my mind' as I witnessed everybody functioning and flowing in their giftings in the environment where they were all 'allowed' to. Since there was no agenda, we never knew what was going to happen. What happened was amazing. I'll tell you about it sometime if you ask me. Like a human body, every single person was of value and necessary for the full health and function.

This experience helped me see that God does not have one person to lead, control, officiate and do all the talking. I can see we are all in one family that can value and respect each individual and seek to encourage each person to share the gold that they have inside them. All can hear

God's voice and repeat what he is saying. All are needed. Every individual is priceless. This has been my 'church' experience since, not in the official buildings, but in houses and pubs, the beach and anywhere that we can have a good natural family time.

From conditional law to unconditional love.

If I could simply summarize my journey of my belief in God, I would say it has been a transition of going from law to love or to put it another way, an awakening to the wonderful realisation that I am being loved unconditionally and am not being judged by conditional law. This is what I mean. It started with the hardcore legalistic, rules, regulations, conditions, prerequisites, stipulations and fear from the law teaching of the first two cults I was in. Trying to conform to this mode of living was like trying to warm death up. Leaving those two places after 30 years has been a gradual awakening to God's love which is diametrically opposed to the conditions of law. Instead of conditions to meet, which is what law demands of you, unconditional love and acceptance revealed my identity of someone who is just loved and accepted. Unless you have experienced this, it will probably appear foolish if not insane. However, as my mind renewed to seeing myself loved unconditionally, something started to happen. Like a bird spreading its wings for the first time, I started to realise that the love I was being shown started to manifest in my life, and was and is, now being sustained by a completely different paradigm than the old law way.

Now, like the currents of wind that keep the bird soaring, the driving power of my life is the realised unconditional love that is inside me, is me and always was me. I was just blinded to it. The more I realise this good news (news is something that has already happened) the more I seem to be able to soar on the wings of love. Without trying to change myself, the more I believe I am loved, the greater capacity I seem to have to give love to another. I can see that to truly live is to love and to truly love is to live. To love unconditionally is true freedom. I have not arrived at this full experience yet and have probably just scratched the surface, but the journey has started. In the last 20 years, I have had numerous nudges and whispers and clues and experiences that have been teaching me about God's unconditional love. One such incredible teaching and another major milestone in my story was a dream which was so vivid that I woke thinking it had literally happened. Here it is:

OUT

My lesson in unconditional love.

In the dream, I was walking down a road. I saw a man on the other side of the road who looked like he was in his early thirties. When I saw this man, I felt hatred towards him even though I didn't know Him. I crossed the road. No one was about. I walked up to the man and punched him hard and knocked him to the ground. He slowly got up, brushed the dust off himself and carried on walking.

I felt the hatred in my heart intensify and I walked up to him again the second time. This time I violently punched and kicked him to the ground. He slowly got up again, didn't retaliate, didn't scowl at me, didn't give me a condemning look. He carried on walking.

This time, I felt a violent rage inside me like a wild beast. I was filled with utter hatred for this man who had done me no harm. I ran up to him and for the third time and I brutally kicked and punched him to the ground, I stamped on him with all my strength. It was an appalling act of violence like I had never seen before, and I was the one doing it! I really hurt him. After a good few minutes, He slowly stood to his feet and turned to me. In obvious great pain he looked at me straight in my eyes and said, "I love you John."

This man who I had hated without a cause, who I had brutally treated and unleashed the rage of violence in me had not retaliated, had not made me feel condemned, had not even defended Himself. He just loved me unconditionally!

Do you know what happened? I broke down sobbing. How could I have hurt such love? How could I have persecuted and brutalised this man of love, without a cause? His love had totally melted the desire to hurt him and had removed the violent desire in me. I couldn't carry on. His love was too strong.

I woke up and was crying my eyes out, filled with love and sorrow at the same time and in awe how that for my worst, I received his best. The man in the dream was Jesus.

How He loves us!

I mean to say, can you possibly imagine someone loving you, accepting you, cherishing you, adoring you, wanting you unconditionally, whatever your condition, with absolutely no conditions, for ten minutes? How about for your whole lifetime? How about for eternity? How would that make you feel? Wouldn't that be the greatest love of all?

Time for a song. You can't talk about this sort of love for too long before you need to sing. How about going straight to your nearest device and playing Billy Joel's Just The Way You Are. As you listen to it, see and feel it through the heart of one who is loving you unconditionally right now.

Since that dream, I have had further encounters with God's love. The God of love and law mixture that I thought he was, was slowly changing from still being a written concept, who you could only access through meeting his terms and conditions, to a living reality of being loved unconditionally freely. In 2012 I was to have three almighty life-changing paradigm shifts that have taken me to where I am today in my belief about God. I won't explain them here but I shall just say what they were. They revealed three massive boulders to me that blocked me from seeing that God truly loves me unconditionally.

1: My relationship, in fact, my perfect union with The Creator, my Father, is never about what I can do or have to do. Instead, it is only ever about what God has done for me. In other words, it is not about me attaining acceptance or status as a Son of God. It is all about me changing my mind (metanoia) to agree that God has already revealed me as his Son. Wow! It is news to believe, not a requirement to earn. As I believe it, I see what has always been true. What a staggering relief from having to attain God's acceptance by conforming to the law that man's religion wants me to bow to. Imagine being free from that and able to totally and utterly and completely accept myself right now because of my identity! He does, so I can too.

2: The above realisation led to this; God has always loved me unconditionally. Always. My life of thinking I was his disappointment, a failure, a continual lawbreaker and just a rebel, led me to think God was barely tolerating me and only really loved me when I was being a 'good' boy. As the realisation dawned on a memorable July night in Edinburgh, it was like living water flushed through my whole life washing away those old fears of withheld love because of my performance. I had always been loved despite my performance.

3: God has never hurt, harmed, stolen, drowned, sliced, wounded, massacred, killed or destroyed anyone ever. I know this will outrage some religious people because of their many seeming rock-solid reasons. I know. They used to be my reasons too why God was a destroying murderer of men, women and children. 'But the Bible says.....' they will say. All I will say here is 'ask the Author.'

So, from the EB days of a God that I believe chained me to a religious system of law, I no longer believe that God is religious. The religious people of the day killed Jesus. Jesus loved them all. I believe two things.

95

OUT

God is right and he is loving me and you right now, perfectly.

At 45 I was to go to Edinburgh for a weekend conference. On the Saturday evening, someone was talking about the whole book of Song of Solomon. During this time Godfrey Birtill, an amazing singer-songwriter, played one of his new songs called 'Two Thousand Years Ago We Bled Into One.'

I happened to be lying flat on my back during this song because I wanted to, and as the words, 'I've always loved you,' were sung I had a 'mind-blowing' epiphany moment. I suddenly could see that throughout my entire life, every day, every situation, every moment, my highest and my lowest of low moments, 'I've always loved you,' had been the heart cry of the Lover of my Soul, my First Love, the one who had revealed his unconditional love to me throughout my life. For the next hour and a half, I was rendered completely drunk on his love and was to stagger around hugging everyone with my eyes shut repeating continually, 'You've always loved me, you've always loved me, you've always loved me.' As this time went on it was like I was seeing a video of my whole life and how even at the many times that I thought God was angry, offended and rejecting me, he was not, he was loving me, he's always loved me. I believe his love is absolutely unconditional.

So what has this chapter got to do with the Exclusive Brethren? Nothing really except that my experiences with a law religion, a knowledge of good and evil religion, a man's religion, a rules and regulations religion, an indoctrinating religion, a controlling religion, has taught me that it's only the unquestioning ego that conforms to all this religious stuff. The 180-degree alternative is knowing that you are unconditionally loved forever. Religion is replaced forever by an unconditional love relationship.

Here is a poem that I wrote as I turned 50 years young. It speaks a lot of where I am today on this great journey of discovery of the greatest love of all...

It's Happening to Me, and You

Hello to you all, you're welcome to listen
to a remarkable fact about me,

OUT

It's taken me years to walk down this path,
that I'm about to invite you to see.
Although it's so personal, as I sketch out this scene,
there's a twist and a paradox or two,
Because while it's about me and my struggle in life,
you'll see it's also about You.

But first, in the context of love,
I have learnt that I must not control,
Or to auto-suggest or put thoughts in your mind,
that might touch your spirit and soul.
I learnt long ago that you've got a free will,
you are allowed to believe what you choose,
So these facts of my life that I offer to you,
are merely for you to peruse.

And peruse it you can, if you will and you'd like to,
and you feel that you want to explore,
I'm not telling you to believe my account,
it's for you to experience and decide for yourself
if there's more.
I'm relaying my finding, or how I was found,
that's a much better way to explain,
It happened like a bolt from the blue,
and in a moment or two,
my life was to be never the same.

I happened to be twelve and had just gone upstairs,
to my bedroom where I was alone,
When all of a sudden, I was immersed in a feeling,
that shook me right through every bone.
I'll try to explain, and this might sound lame
but, imagine standing under a hot waterfall.
A torrent of love is streaming right through your heart,
sounds like a passionate call.

Imagine feeling wanted and needed and adored,
accepted and loved, all at the same time,
Imagine feeling cherished and special and one of a kind
and perfectly safe and sublime,

OUT

Imagine being the apple of the eye, embraced by perfection
and belonging and fitting like a glove,
And knowing that this feeling was a reality,
knowing that I am unconditionally loved.

Imagine if all thought of rejection and fear,
was suddenly tsunami'd away,
Imagine if feeling that now all that mattered,
was to love and to live every day,
And be free without judgment of self or another,
no need to live from the past,
But to live in each moment and see through the eyes
of eternal love, from the first, to the last.

Now, fast forward thirty-eight years to today,
cause since, I'll tell you, it's been one hell of a ride,
A stormy voyage of distractions and minefields,
up against the fierce battle with my pride,
Controlled by man's religions of law,
told what to believe, swallowing cunning philosophies of fear,
Straight-jacketed by men who took over my life
and threatened that if I didn't meet conditions,
eternal damnation was near,

I could go on, but you get the idea,
I took my eyes off my First Love,

I fell for the lie that I had to be good enough,
that Love was way way far above,
...or somewhere way below,
so I spent many years fighting a futile waste,
Forgetting that perfect love never leaves nor forsakes,
never changes, whatever the case.

And here is the mystery,
the point of why I'm offering you this story,
This Love that's inside each and every one of us,
is Christ in you, the hope of glory,
No matter what we feel or where our life is going,
whether it's you or it's me,

OUT

We are all being perfectly loved right now,
always were,
always will be,
throughout time and then,
for all eternity.

JDS 2016

Chapter 13

I'd like you to know how I got healed because...

there is hope for everybody

Do you, or does anyone you know, need healing from past or present bad religious experiences?

Maybe you were in a cult and still feel the rejection from the people you once knew so well? Maybe you are still wounded by the control and false authority that once ruled or is still ruling your life? Maybe you find it so hard to forgive yourself for wasting so many years in deception? Maybe you are separated from your parents and loved ones and still harbour strong feelings of bitterness and frustration? No matter how old and deep the wounds may be, whatever healing is needed, my prayer is that you will receive it and be able to move onwards in joy and peace and live the rest of your life free from the grip of the past. As you read this chapter, see if any aspects of my experiences could be useful to yourself or someone you know.

I realise how serious and sensitive this subject is. We are talking here about the quality of life for a human individual. Can a price be put on that quality of life for every individual? Nowadays our society goes to great lengths to protect and care for one another. What would life look like with no health service, no police, no army, no health and safety, no schools or welfare benefit? Well, what about the millions of people that are suffering to various degrees with abuse, wounds and scars arising from religion? How is help going to come? Who cares?

I have been incredibly fortunate over the years to have received significant elements of healing from my past. One of the hallmarks of my healing was when the past stopped being a daily part of my thinking and the point came when I found I could talk about those years freely to anyone without any feelings of hurt, entrapment or dread. When I think of my parents, I have a smile and lightness in my heart. When I think of the members still in the cult, I only feel compassion and sadness for them all. Their leader put a wall between them and me. I found a way to forgive him. From my perspective, there is no wall.

I have grown in self-respect and confidence; no longer just a doormat or under the control of man. I have become acutely aware of honouring my free will and yours too. The confusion of the past appears to have been replaced with an exceptionally helpful understanding of why it all happened.

I have learnt to accept people and 'allow' them to be themselves without judging them. I no longer think 'I am right.' Wow! That needs another book of itself, maybe called 'I Am Wrong.' Nowadays I am at peace regarding the Exclusive Brethren and above all, I have every reason to love everybody unconditionally. I am not claiming to have fully arrived at any of these things, but I sure am enjoying the journey.

Healing for me came in three main parts:

1.   Acceptance of the grief and loss of losing my loving parents came through the experience of what is often known as the 'five stages of death.'

2.   Unconditional forgiveness towards the EB system and the Leader, who prescribed the laws that split my family and controlled us, which came through an amazing dream.

3.   The awakening to the power of love that came through realising that I am totally loved and accepted unconditionally by God.

1: The Five Stages of Death

When a person leaves a cult for whatever reason, it can be like experiencing a type of death. Even if you are the one that deliberately escaped believing that getting out was the best thing for you, letting go of those closely-knit bonds and the familiarity and belonging, follows a similar process as mourning a death.

Elisabeth Kübler-Ross created the Five Stages of Death theory of which the principles can be applied to many different aspects of loss in someone's life. The stages are not prescriptive, and the order and time scale can differ in each person and in every situation. Generally speaking, the principles can help bring an understanding and aid the healing process to an experience of any type of loss. In my 'cult escape,' the loss I had to come to terms with was not the actual leaving of the EB. I had long given up on keeping all their laws, and in my view, that whole spiritually abusive package required a different type of healing. I recognise these five stages in my healing process just applied to the traumatic loss of my parents who I knew I might never see again.

Here is the way I see these five stages outworked in my particular experience. They started the moment I entered my apartment on the day that I left home. It was at this moment that it finally hit me. I had escaped. I was free. But I had lost my parents. I cried continuously for three hours during which the following thought processes occurred:

1: Denial – I was in shock. I was with my parents half an hour ago. I had been with them from birth. Surely that has not come to an end. Surely, I have not really left them. We are together really.

This then moved into the second stage and so on;

2: Anger – Why have I had to go through this impossible situation? Why have I had to make an impossible choice? How dare I be cornered in such a way! How dare my life turn out this way!

3: Blame – From what I remember, I irrationally blamed the imaginary deck of cards that had been stacked against me causing my life to come to this point.

4: Depression – What is the point of life? How can I go on feeling like this? I can't imagine ever feeling any different. I feel like I have had to shoot my parents and bury them under the patio. This is the last thing I wanted to ever do. They are distraught. I made my Mum cry. My Dad felt trapped. They have lost two sons now. This is just awful. This is impossible.

As the three hours went by and I just let it all out without any restraint, my extreme emotions seemed to take me through these four stages and I began to see and feel that these four feelings; denial, anger, blame and depression were not answers. Of themselves, they were just deep feelings I was experiencing. They were revealers of the reality, or should

I say, my present reality, my transitioning reality even. The weeping seemed to exhaust each stage. I seemed to experience each emotion until I had seen and felt them from every angle. It was as though these emotions had been hidden in the dark and the weeping gradually exposed them all to light enabling me to see and understand them. As I said, they were not answers. When I saw them for what they were, they weakened and gradually lost their sting.

It took me three hours by which time a new feeling was to emerge, and I remember thinking these exact words and making a strong commitment.

'I don't like these feelings. They are very depressing. I am not going to carry on like this. I can't change the past. I am going to the video shop to get some comedy videos.'

I had reached number 5: Acceptance – I came to the place where I knew that denial, anger, blame and depression were never going to help me. It seemed that I had cried them out of my system. I saw them for what they are. They would only keep me down, control me and destroy me. In one sense, they were not my friends. They were just pointers to the journey that I must take to get free. They were not going to set me free. My coming to acceptance of these facts enabled me to see that though I can't change the past, life truly goes on. I wasn't living in my past. I accepted my lot. I was now living in the present.

A wave of hope flushed through me. Not hope for the past because that was gone but hope for now and the future. I went to the local video shop on Lawrence Road, Wavertree and hired Fawlty Towers and Laurel and Hardy. I watched them, laughed and have been laughing ever since. Why not? The sunny side of the street is always there. If it's cloudy the sun is still there above the clouds. Clouds come to pass. There's no point in crying over spilt milk. More so, there's no point in crying over milk that hasn't been spilt. Why bang my head against a brick wall? These were some of the early metaphors that helped me choose the positive reality to my life. It appears that those extreme three hours fast-forwarded me into acceptance. If so then I am very fortunate. I've heard that some people take years to work through those stages. Having knowledge of the five stages can enable you to understand a natural process and can help you to be courageous during this time before you come out of the other side. Many who apply the five stages to their own loss find it helps them move faster through their situation. If you are going through a loss right now, can you identify a stage you might be at? Everyone is different.

2: The dream that shattered my unforgiveness.

I have had educational dreams all through my life; each one seemed so real, that even today, I still feel like I have lived through the experiences. Here is the dream I had about 15 years ago which taught me how and why I can choose to forgive and free myself from unforgiveness.

In the dream, I call round to Tommy's house. He was an old friend of 20 years and we often played cricket together. His mother answered the door. I asked her if Tommy was playing out. She looked me in the eyes and slowly and deliberately said to me, 'Tommy wants me to tell you that he never wants to play cricket with you, ever again.'

I am shocked and stunned. How those words stung me. We were great friends and had been for 20 years. There had never been a bad word spoken between us. In that moment of feeling so hurt, so rejected, so let down, so mistreated, I think, 'How could he be so nasty? How could he say such a thing to me? What a cruel thing to say to a friend.' I feel the pain of anger, resentment and rejection start to build up.

Seeing the confusion and hurt on my face, Tommy's Mother continued. 'Last night Tommy was in a car accident and has lost all his limbs.'

Let that sink in!

The truth was revealed. Poor Tommy was incapable of playing cricket. He was disabled. He was incapacitated. Think about those strong feelings I had just been having of hurt, rejection, being let down and being mistreated by Tommy. Stop! It wasn't Tommy's fault. He was utterly incapable of playing cricket. Instead of those negative feelings towards him and my feeling sorry for myself, I see a totally different perspective and feel immensely sorry for Tommy. I feel total compassion and of course not one shred of blame. No longer am I holding against him, his wishes to never play cricket with me again.

I woke up from the dream and could instantly see how this teaching related to my relationship with the members of the Exclusive Brethren. Instead of feeling bitter, resentful, angry and blaming them for the controlling laws and the separation of my family, I only felt compassion, understanding and love for them all.

This is because my perspective now saw them disabled, very dis-abled. I saw them as incapable of seeing their life in any other way while they followed their idol, their so-called 'Man of God'. The brainwashing and fear had rendered them incapacitated. How can I hold anything against them? They can't help what they are doing. Understanding this, I found and find forgiveness easy and natural and compassion has replaced any negativity towards them all. Simultaneously I remembered a Bible verse I had heard hundreds of times in the EB from Jesus' last words on the cross, when he said, 'Father, forgive them, for they know not what they do.' I could see the parallel.

Could this understanding, if we want it to, apply to everyone and anyone who has ever wronged us in any way shape or form? This dream helped me realise a massive part of my healing from my EB days. I am at peace with everyone there and it helps me forgive myself too.

3: Realising that I am totally loved and accepted unconditionally by God.

This third aspect of my healing, that I have identified, blows the other two out of the water in comparison. It was like it was revealed to me and I know this will sound outrageous but here goes; I discovered the power of the universe; Unconditional Love.

Now, I start to get a bit passionate about this subject. It is all relevant to this chapter and my healing, so bear with me please.

Just consider this. You may not believe in God or think you have any faith. I am not trying to change your mind. I can't. However, what is undeniable is that the actions of people follow what they believe. The old proverb says, 'As a man thinks in his heart, so is he.' What a person believes makes them the person they are. Every culture, religion, era, philosophy and plain common sense observe this reality. If you believe in your heart that you are love you will love. If you believe in your heart that you are hate you will hate. Whatever you sow in your heart you will reap in your life. Your life will reflect and correlate to what you believe.

Here's a massive question. Read this slowly. If we are what we believe, what could be the highest, greatest, ultimate pinnacle of what it is possible, that you and I, or any human can believe? Jesus once said, 'If you can believe, all things are possible to him who believes.'

OUT

So the question is, what is the highest possible belief that we could ever have? May I suggest to you that the answer is simple. The answer is love. If this world was to believe that their true identity was love and therefore change their self-image to love because we are what we believe, this is what this world would change to;

People of all races would be connected,
Slavery and inhumane acts would stop,
All reason behind war would dry up,
People would be accepting of one another's differences,
Stealing, greed and power-mongering would lose its appeal,
Locksmiths would go out of business,
Resources would be spent on feeding the world instead of making weapons,
The norm would be friendliness, warmth, kindness and goodwill to all mankind,
The planet and all of nature would be respected and cared for,
We would all put the needs of our neighbour first,
There would be no divided religion. Love would be the only religion...
and... by believing that we are love, we would be healed from our past wounds and scars.

The reason I am saying all this is because the single biggest reason I put my overall healing down to, is my awakening that I am being unconditionally loved and that this love is inside me too. I believe this. In fact, I believe it is my true identity. As I began to realise and grow in this belief, fear, anxiety, resentment, frustration, pain and any negativity from my past seemed to disperse just like mist in the early morning sun. I started to see the past, present and future in a new light, a light of understanding, compassion, acceptance, forgiveness and mercy.

It changed my whole perspective on people, including the EB. I found that I was at peace with my past. No longer was I a victim. I was free to love and from this perspective, from this belief, I discovered such powerful healing that as I said before, the past has stopped being a part of my daily thinking and I am free to talk about it without any fearful feelings at all.

This wonderful healing is the result of believing that I am being

unconditionally loved.

SHAKE IT ALL ABOUT

CHAPTER 14

Why write Cult Escape?

the motivation

What is the big deal about religious cults? What makes many people so interested in learning about what goes on in such groups of human beings? Is it because of the peculiar ways that some people choose to live their lives? Is it because it is intriguing how so many people actually believe they are right and everyone else is wrong? Is it because some cults can be very dangerous and harmful to individuals and families?

Did you know, that unlike slave trafficking, for example, leading a religious cult or being a member, of itself, is not illegal. So, what do you do if you believe that people are indoctrinated into a religious belief system, that is damaging to themselves and their families? What if you were one of those people?

One thing you cannot do is coerce or manipulate people into changing their mind, because that would be overriding their free will. That's what controlling cults do. People have a choice in life and that must be respected. One thing you can do is write your personal story about what you experienced, make your observations and share your perspectives openly and honestly. Then whoever is feeling trapped in their 'religion', whoever wants to examine all they have been taught by their leader and traditions, and whoever is willing to consider freedom from cult law, they then may feel they have a better opportunity to do so.

When I started writing this book, I questioned my motives. I wanted to know why I was writing it. What was the real reason? Did I have an agenda? Did I want to attack the people from my past? Did I want to settle a grievance? Did I want to get something out of my system?

It was for none of these reasons. When I eventually got to listening to my heart, I realised that I wasn't writing the book:

- To have a go at any individual or group.
- To coerce anyone into leaving the cultic system they are in.
- To get cults shut down by the government.
- To promote conditional love.

Simply, I was writing:

1: To inspire courage and hope for anyone who seeks freedom from religious control.

2: To point towards healing and wholeness for those who are suffering psychologically after having their lives and families torn apart by cult law.

3: To warn the world about religious cults and what could happen if people were ever to ever join one.

4: To shine a bit of unconditional love into this world.

The tipping point to writing this book came when I turned 50 years old. Out of the blue it seemed, compassion rose up in me for the many people trapped under religious law. I felt a strong sense of responsibility. I knew personally about religious entrapment but had been doing nothing about it. I knew many people whose families have been split up by religious law and the torment and trauma that causes. The memories of the terrible struggle for freedom that I went through and knowing that many are going through the same struggles, compelled me to take action. So, I wrote my story with the corresponding website resource.

So why write the book now, over 30 years after leaving the Exclusive Brethren?

Someone asked me if I want to destroy the EB. "Certainly not," I replied, "I just feel that it is fair for people to get to know their options in life so that they can freely choose if they want to."

I now realise that I wasn't ready until now. There was a vital ingredient missing. Without this ingredient I would just be pulling down, attacking and going to war. I needed to realise the love inside me first. That love had to overflow so that rather than a criticism, I would have a solution, a way forward to unity and love for all.

Through this book I want people to know that they are not trapped in any system that man tells them they have to stay in. I see that we are all worth more than being treated like a pawn in somebody else's chess game. Although getting free from a cult is not easy, there is hope. There are other options in life. There are better perspectives and values to realise. There is a more excellent way. There is love; unconditional love.

There are escape routes to freedom from the crushing laws of controlling man's religions of fear. There is knowledge to be realised that can set you free. There are people who can help. Healing is an option you can discover and peace can be arrived at in your mind. There is more to life than 'this.' New values can be recognised resulting in life-changing motivation. Love will conquer all. It is a great journey knowing that love never fails.

To control and put laws on people is not love. To close down a mind to only believe what you are saying, is not love. Coercive control is not love. To put burdens on people that are too heavy for them to bear is not love. To instil fearful beliefs into families, should they follow their loved ones when they leave, is not love. To change the goalposts then split families if they don't conform to your laws is not love. To excommunicate and shun people who break your laws, then deny you have a responsibility in their split family, is not love. To allow yourself to be subject to these things is not loving yourself.

This book is not written just for those who have been affected by the cult I was born into. There are literally thousands of religious cults in this world. Most people have only heard of the prominent ones. Cult Escape is a pointer to all religious organisations which exert control over their followers. The control within these groups ranges from mild to extreme. My hope is that a world-wide awakening to the dangers of cult indoctrination and brainwashing will increase, creating a shift away from family separation, wars, disrespect, control and division, and instead, encouraging the move towards a society that is growing in respect, unity and love towards one another.

This is why I wrote this book.

CHAPTER 15

Do religious cults split up families?

they all say no!

In my view, one of the most inhumane acts committed by people is when they split up families; husbands from wives, parents from children or grandparents from families, any family member for that matter, by putting religious laws in their way that cause this unspeakable division and separation, then justify it all in the name of their god.

It was such laws that my parents were under when I left the Exclusive Brethren system in 1988. I wanted to be able to have a 'normal life' with them, but their Man of God laws said that they must separate themselves from me, also from their parents, from their siblings, from their nephews and nieces who had also left the system.

I want to emphasise that although I am using my experiences in the Exclusive Brethren in this chapter, the points made also relate to any organisation with beliefs that ultimately lead to the splitting up of families. However, I've yet to find a cult that admits that they do. See what you think.

Separation versus Union
The Exclusive Brethren's identity was rooted in a very extreme core

doctrine that came from their first prominent leader, J.N. Darby. In 1847 he wrote a pamphlet describing it with his title, Separation from Evil, God's Principle of Unity.

This doctrine simply means that to be in unity with God, according to the EB, you had to separate yourself from what and how the current Man of God defined as evil. The Man of God's definitions were law. To follow this man now meant you were under law, his law. This principle still pervades several of the Brethren denominations and various other cults to this day.

There is a blind spot to this principle. It is simply that all followers believe that the Man of God's particular interpretation of what is 'evil' is the correct one. They believe that to live a life that is righteous and acceptable to God, they have to make judgements based on the knowledge of good and evil as instructed by the Man of God. Despite changes in law over time, all believe they have the correct version at each point in time, despite the obvious evolution of their current 'truth.' This is a blind spot because you will find that most are indoctrinated or brainwashed into believing that their version alone is correct, and are therefore incapable of even allowing a contrary thought to enter their thinking.

Let me illustrate. Many who are reading this right now may concede that the blind spot is true of other denominations, sects and cults but not theirs. It is easy to compare other beliefs with ours and see how others are 'clearly in error'. However, the last thing to enter our mind is, could I also be in error, in delusion, in falsehood and blindly following a 'Man of God', Guru, Teacher, Master or Leader? No! Surely not! As an Exclusive Brethren member once said to me, "We don't need to ask God about any alternative because we know we are in the right position."

The irony is that a far more realistic title for J.N. Darby's doctrine should have been Separation from Evil, Darby's Principle of DISUNITY, for the reality is that it has been the basis of repeated schisms that have splintered the Brethren movement into many discordant fragments and split up countless people from each other over the decades.

In reality, the separation that we practised amounted to separating ourselves from anyone who disagreed with us, which meant anyone who disagreed with our Leader.

Incidentally, you will not find in the Bible any verse that says separation is God's principle of unity, but there is one that says in effect that LOVE is God's principle of unity. Colossians 3:14 says "Above all, clothe yourselves with love, which binds everything together in perfect harmony."

A tree is known by its fruit and I have seen over fifty years of the fruit from this most heinous doctrine that 'separation from evil is God's principle of unity.' I do not believe it is. In my experience and view, the fruit is rotten to the core. I have seen that tree produce fear, self-righteousness, pride, legalism, suspicion, division, elitism, bigotry, exclusivism, ungodly separation of families, false separation, isolation, hatred, condemnation and counting all who aren't of 'our righteous views' as unworthy of our company.

Important Note: It wasn't those who left who wanted their family split up. It was those remaining in the EB, who valued their Man of God's laws higher than family, causing and maintaining separation. When I left, I left the system, not the people, but the laws of the EB meant that my family and everyone was split from me.

73% versus 0%.
When I left the Exclusive Brethren in 1988 there were about two hundred members in the Liverpool group which is where I lived. In writing this chapter I wanted to discover how many members were in families that were split up. So, I made a list of all the people who I could remember which was 152. To my shock, I realised that 112 of them were in families that were split up. That is 73%. This is a verifiable fact. The EB law dictated that whoever stayed a member, had to separate / split / divide themselves from anyone who left. Do you know anyone whose family is split because of religious law?

To try to put this 73% of members in split families into some sort of context, I then did a survey of local churches near where I live. The question was how many people's families were split as a direct result of their 'church law,' (I.e. law that the church leader with his power could enforce, instructing members to split their families if one or more should disobey him).

Out of 800 local church members, I found that 0% had a split family due to their church law.

SHAKE IT ALL ABOUT

No one disagrees that most of the EB members are in families that are 'split up'. These people who we were 'split up' from were classified as being 'evil,' 'worldly,' 'unclean,' 'wrong,' 'unrighteous,' 'disobedient,' 'not worthy of our fellowship,' and many other negative things.

Since the inception of the Exclusive Brethren, there are thousands of people whose families have been 'split up.' They once lived together as a family. Now they live separate lives. Who decided it? Who did it?

First of all, let's look at the definition of 'split up':

'Split up' is a state a family is in when at least one of the family members are not allowed to spend 'normal family time' together. They are separated from one another. The family is 'split up.' They are divided.

Definition of 'normal family time' is where:

- Families are allowed and free to live together if desired.
- Families are allowed and free to visit each other in their homes and stay with each other.
- Families are allowed to freely celebrate the birth of their grandchildren and family weddings.
- Families are allowed to fully join in freely with the funeral arrangements of family members.
- Families are allowed to freely celebrate birthdays and special occasions.
- Families are allowed to eat or drink freely with each other anywhere.
- Families are allowed to freely go out shopping together.
- Families are allowed to freely go on holidays together.

Now, I want to draw your attention to the following fact. Under the first three leaders of the EB who were Darby, Raven and Taylor Senior, families were generally allowed to do everything on the above list. Even if they may have been withdrawn from, their families were not 'split up' and normal family life was kept intact. The fact is that something changed.

What changed?

The laws changed.

Whose laws?

The Exclusive Brethrens' laws.

Who changed and made the laws?

The current Man of God at the time.

SHAKE IT ALL ABOUT

When I was an EB member, the reason (or excuse) that the EB gave, as to why they didn't 'split up' families, was that they said that people chose to leave themselves. 'It was nothing to do with us,' they would say. My older brother physically walked out as soon as he was 16 because he couldn't keep all the religious laws imposed upon him. He told me that the EB never contacted him again. So, while it is true that anyone can physically leave at any time, you have to look at the big picture to really see what was going on. The following illustrates how religious family separation happens:

1: A family is united, joined by their love, their marriage and their birthright. Grandparents, parents, children, uncles, aunts and cousins. One family.

2: A cult leader with influence and power over that family instructs them to obey his laws/rules. He gets them so indoctrinated that they will virtually do anything he tells them to do. They believe he is either God himself, or God's spokesman. There are serious consequences should he be disobeyed. (Note: this is what is happening today in thousands of cults across the world.)

3: Examples of various cult laws: You have to be an accepted member. You can't smoke, you can't go into a bar, you can't have a mobile phone, you have to sign your will and finances over to the group, you have to give 10% of your income, you can't have a blood transfusion, you can't drink coffee, you can't have a television, you can't have a computer, you can only live in a detached house, you can't sleep in hotels, you can't go abroad on holidays, you can only marry who the leader approves of, you can't have a moustache, you can't wear a bikini on the beach, and you can't have a cup of tea with your neighbour who is not in your group etc etc.

4: Some cult followers find that for many different reasons, they cannot bear the burdens of the laws/rules that their leader has influence and power over them to enforce. They reach a breaking point where they fail to keep the laws/rules and end up getting 'split off' from their loving families. They don't leave because they want to get away from their families. They love their families but the EB laws meant whoever left had to be separated from, and the result was the family was split up.

Important note repeated: It wasn't those who left who wanted their family split up. It was those remaining in the EB, who valued their laws higher than family, causing and maintaining separation.

An example of this is someone I know, who was withdrawn from about ten years ago. His family never visit him and he does not even know where his wife lives. He told me that his door is always open for his family to be with him, but they don't visit. Why not? Because they are maintaining a position of separation. He isn't, they are. They are obeying their religious laws resulting in their family split.

Another example is my personal situation. My family have not visited me since I left almost 30 years ago. I would love to share my life with them, and my door is always open to them. They also would love us all to be together. We all love each other. What is stopping them? It is the family-splitting religious laws as dictated by their leader that prevents them. They fear the consequences of breaking the laws they are under.

The effects on people who lose their loved ones to cult law.

I invite you to stop and think what it must be like, facing the prospect of never seeing your family again. Many have experienced this with the death of a single loved one. When this happens, people go through immense grief and sorrow that can affect them for the rest of their lifetime.

Now imagine this happening to a loved one who is still alive and well, yet is under cult law. They are separated from you simply because the cultic religious law they have been coerced into believing, has forbidden them from continuing to live with you or maintain a normal family life.

What was once a happy united family is now divided. The dynamic has changed. You are no longer welcome like you used to be. You do not belong anymore. There is a barrier between your Mother or your Father or your siblings and you. You cannot hug and kiss them anymore. They are not allowed to. They ostracise you and just engage in small talk if you phone them up.

This living death situation can traumatise a person and to different extents it does. The natural bonds are broken, the familial relationships are smashed. Why? Because a man is holding your loved ones by laws that he has convinced them to value higher, than living with you. Love for his law is greater to them than their love for you.

This is just a snippet of the disruption, trauma, rejection and despair that thousands of ex-cult members have gone through and still cope with on a daily basis. A split family can cause more suffering than literal death because it is like living death. The loved ones are there but cannot be connected with. Many find no way to get over it and move on. I have spoken to many who are still deeply troubled after decades. Why? Because a cult leader is controlling their loved ones, holding them in a grip of fear. The effects cannot be measured as everyone is different. Some commit suicide, some never get over it, some stay traumatised for decades, only a few it seems get healed.

Do religious cults split up families? You decide.

CHAPTER 16

Examining Indoctrination and Brainwashing

two main cultic hallmarks

What if we were to shine a light on the meanings and implications of these two words and..... you were to realise, that you have spent many years of your life, either indoctrinated or brainwashed?

How would you feel? I reckon many people might well by-pass this chapter, just in case.

By examining these words, it will become apparent where indoctrination or brainwashing is happening, what potential effects there are and how people can choose to think for themselves and not just be a puppet under man's control. Understanding these words can shed light on what might have happened to you or someone you know, how it might have happened and why it happened.

Quick point to consider; Religious cults don't admit that indoctrination or brainwashing takes place in their group.

First, a brief definition of these two words.

Indoctrination is either: (1) any form of teaching aimed at getting students to adopt beliefs independent of the evidential support those beliefs may have (or lack); (2) any form of teaching based on methods that instil beliefs in students in such a way that they are unwilling or unable to question or evaluate those beliefs independently; or (3) any form of teaching that causes students to embrace a specific set of beliefs—e.g., a certain political ideology or a religious doctrine—without regard for its evidential status. (1)

(1) Harvey Siegel, "Philosophy of education," Encyclopaedia Britannica, 2018, www.britannica.com/topic/philosophy-of-education#ref936431

Brainwashing, also called Coercive Persuasion, is a systematic effort to persuade nonbelievers to accept a certain allegiance, command, or doctrine. A colloquial term, it is more generally applied to any technique designed to manipulate human thought or action against the desire, will, or knowledge of the individual. By controlling the physical and social environment, an attempt is made to destroy loyalties to any unfavourable groups or individuals, to demonstrate to the individual that his attitudes and patterns of thinking are incorrect and must be changed, and to develop loyalty and unquestioning obedience to the ruling party. (2)

(2)   The Editors of Encyclopaedia Britannica, "Brainwashing," Encyclopaedia Britannica, 2018,
https://www.britannica.com/topic/brainwashing

Simply put, Indoctrination instils in you a new belief. Brainwashing, which includes indoctrination, changes your current belief to another belief. The results are the same. The person who has been indoctrinated or brainwashed will fall for the will of the teacher and become a slave to their control and desires.

What is the difference between education and indoctrination?
The following quote illustrates this clearly.

'The difference between education and indoctrination is that education opens the mind, while indoctrination closes it. Education is a process-driven approach to engaging in the knowledge and ideas of the world. Education is playful, experimental, mysterious. Education opens doors of intellectual exploration and equips its students with the tools they will need to dissect, analyse, and interpret the information that they find.

Indoctrination, on the other hand, is a results-driven approach that aims to instil in people a set of habits and beliefs that align with an ideology or political agenda. Indoctrination narrows the lens through which we are able to see the world and ensures that all of the information we receive is interpreted through the filter of the promoted ideology.' (5)

(5)   Jonah Canner, "Education or Indoctrination?" IDEA: The Institute for Democratic Education in America, 2010), http://www.democraticeducation.org/index.php/blog/article/education_or_indoctrination/

Let's examine indoctrination and brainwashing in the light of my own experience. Since I was born into the EB, I never knew anything different. According to the above definitions, I wouldn't say I was brainwashed. However, in my opinion, the whole lifestyle meant that I was indoctrinated, and controlled into believing the whole EB then current laws and doctrines, from a child, which included:

- Separation from evil was God's principle of unity, as defined by the Man of God's latest version of 'evil.'
- The Man of God was the Universal Leader, the Leader of the Recovery of the Truth, the Elect Vessel, the spiritual descendant of Paul and whatever he said, is what God was saying.
- When people violated the will of the Man of God, it was a good thing that they were cut off, for life if necessary, because they were unclean like a leper.
- We alone had the truth. We certainly didn't know anyone else who did.
- Everyone outside of the EB was of the world and therefore unclean and unworthy to eat with us.
- The Man of God's interpretations of the Bible were the right ones. All others were wrong.
- Whenever the Man of God introduced a new law or rule, even one that contradicted the previous law, it was always justified because we were told that "God had turned a corner".

As a result of this indoctrination, I grew up thinking and believing that:

- My four grandparents, two uncles and aunts and ten cousins were unclean, wicked and of the devil and it would be totally wrong to have any contact with them. (This was because from 1970 when I was four years old, these relatives were 'withdrawn from' and therefore completely cut off and we were not allowed to have any more contact.
- Attending eleven meetings, latterly ten a week was essential to maintain obedience to what the Man of God expected us all to do.
- Sharing a meal with literally anyone who wasn't an EB member, even having a cup of tea with a neighbour, was a wicked sin.
- Anyone who wasn't an EB member was 'worldly,' 'unclean,'

'ignorant,' 'wrong,' 'unrighteous,' 'disobedient,' 'not worthy of our fellowship,' amongst other things.

- Houses that had shared drains or adjoining walls were of the 'world' and not separate.
- Televisions were a "pipeline of filth" and to even physically touch one was a sinful act.
- Computers, mobile phones, radios, recorded music was all evil and 'worldly.'
- Cinemas, theatres, sporting events or any entertainment was of the world and absolutely 'worldly.'
- Owning a pet was 'worldly' and took away our affection from God.
- Funfairs, theme parks or circuses were 'worldly' and all people going to these places were deceived.
- Joining trade unions, any unions or having a job where you must sign the Secrecy Act, was evil as it meant having a link with the world.
- Doing jury service was to share in making a judgement with the 'world' and was forbidden.
- Men having sideburns, moustaches or hair that wasn't short was 'worldly.'
- Women who wore makeup or jewellery, wore trousers or dyed or cut their hair short were 'worldly.'

I was immersed daily in an environment of these beliefs. Eleven meetings a week forged the neural pathways in my mind so deep that I grew up a clone to the dictates of the Leader. I believe I was literally disabled from critical thinking and analysis. There was only one thought, one truth and that was we were 'right.' This attitude and false identity formed crusts of layers of internal fear of ever stepping over the line, confusion as to who I really was, paranoia about the possibility I might go to hell, and a deep dread of ever being separated from my family.

Apart from the hellfire indoctrination, I rate the worst of these as being the harsh, judgemental, despising and looking down on people who weren't in the 'truth,' like we were. I remember our neighbours two doors away who we learnt were Catholics. I remember having feelings of hatred in my heart against these 'stinky Catholics' who didn't have truth that we had. I was probably about 5 years old. Sorry Catholics, I love you all now. Looking back, I am amazed just how screwed up I was.

Brainwashing, the cousin of Indoctrination.

Those who are born into a cultic group are gradually indoctrinated from childhood in the cult's belief system. People who get brainwashed are those who tend to join a cult as an adult, and they get their belief system changed through repetition, information withheld, and pressure to conform through direct force or indirect psychological force using fear.

'Brainwashing' is a generic term that some academics believe is nebulous, absolves people of their responsibility and has no scientific basis. I do not share this viewpoint. I believe it is valid and a very useful word which explains much cultic behaviour. When someone who has been brainwashed gets to understand what has happened to them, it can bring great healing to that person. The degree to how much a person gets brainwashed can vary, just as control and manipulation can vary, but this does not invalidate the term in my view. Also, what is the social perception of what brainwashing is? I took to social media LinkedIn platform to find out by asking the following question:

"In its simplest form, can you tell me what the term brainwashing means to you?"

I was quite surprised by the detailed responses: The following are all the comments by people that answered the question. All were asked if they wanted their name or initials included. Some wanted to remain anonymous:

1.   Brainwashing for me means being influenced into believing a particular set of beliefs, views are correct over all others to the point where a person loses the critical thinking and desire to challenge them as they are now an absolute truth. This influencing can easily come from and individual as well as an organisation. Dave Verburg

2.   To me, it would be changing/influencing somebody's mind into them thinking they have no power & must follow a certain way? Aumair Khalid

3.   For me, brainwashing means you that are being so subsumed in conditioning messages that you are being conditioned or tricked into a belief that you previously did not believe and likely would never have believed if presented with more balanced information. When associated with cults I also perceive that threats of force, violence or other consequence are also used to

enforce that set of beliefs on someone. Though I don't believe the force, violence is always present. For example, I think we are brainwashed by our mainstream press. Jo S

4. Brainwashing is to make a person have a limited belief of the world. The brainwashed person can only consume information which is given by the brainwasher. You have no free will of the use of your own analytical thinking or thought process. You must follow the rules given and will do so after long term conditioning because you know nothing else and this becomes your reality. Murilyn

5. Yes, I was brainwashed to believe that the world would end in 1975. That was the belief of the fundamentalist cult, Jehovah's Witnesses, now receiving unwelcome publicity in the form of the film, Apostasy. Brian Hunt

6. Animal farm springs to mind... That's why kids should be encouraged to read widely and develop their own critical thinking capabilities... Steve Rigby

7. For me, brainwashing is to control the persons' perception of the reality which is far away from reality. It is the worst form of emotional abuse and pain. I have never met with such abuse in real life apart from reading about it. Katarzyna Machalinski

8. To me, it means trying to get others to act the way one wants no matter what. Anon

9. Brainwashing is someone or a group or a religious sect or govt continually forcing a doctrine or way of thinking on an individual. Very often this does not allow alternative views from this message. Mike Holmes

10. To me, it means being psychologically manipulated. Aiden Murray

11. Brainwashing is what propaganda does to you. While it may not be "scientific", it's certainly understood. Michal

12. It is a manipulation of people's mind to accept once opinion as the only one truth. Keeping people from thinking for themselves. I recently was talking to a girl that wants to study to be a nurse. Her congregation kicked her out because it was against the rules. How crazy that is. Thankfully she is a smart girl and will go to follow her dream. Ganka Wolbers

13. It means being made to believe something without question when that thing isn't actually true or correct. Pam Case

14. People taking on beliefs of others that they may not wish to have.

SHAKE IT ALL ABOUT

Bob Evans

15. Brainwashing to me suggests repeated reinforcement of a message, whether positive or negative, without consideration of any alternate views. Kris M

16. Subliminally or forced conversion by manipulation to alter the view or beliefs of an individual. Emma Preston

17. Yes, I think we all have a clear perception of what this means, and it's also self-explanatory too. I see it as manipulation of another's mind for some self-benefit. Christina Smith

18. We are all being brainwashed all the time - it's called the advertising industry and the media! It teaches us what to think and feel, and it's right there in the centre of our home, on the buses and trains to work, on the airwaves in our cars. It's everywhere. When they set out on a campaign to vilify a section of our community, a behaviour or whatever, people just jump on board with these things because they haven't learned how to think independently or to ask questions when something doesn't feel right. What religious cults do is tap into that tendency, create fears in the minds of people and then draw them in with promises of safety and security from the big bad world outside. As Thoreau puts it, the mass of men lead lives of quiet desperation, and that's what is played upon by the ones who've figured out how to think outside the mass media, but then use it to manipulate people for their own selfish ends, while making those same people feel guilty and ashamed for wanting the same for themselves! Tania A

19. Being told something again and again until you believe it regardless of its truth. Chris Barnes

20. Hmm, brainwashing, is when we are drilled with a same message constantly since young and that we are constantly being told that we have to do things this way, and that we should only listen to that one thing/one person - it's also being heavily under influence of a person with that certain message. And without going into specifics, it's a mindset that has been indoctrinated since young and we end up growing up without exposure to anything else, or to the outside world. More often than not, it is very hard to change that mindset of that person whom we think could have been 'brainwashed', unless they are willing to take the first step into the unknown (to them). JC

21. It's about being told something repeatedly for so long that you

believe it without question. Paul Corcoran

22. Manipulation of one's thoughts in the main. And belittling one asking any questions. Anon

23. Brainwashing is convincing someone that they have absolutely no power, then using them for your own purposes. CG

24. I think it's a valid word as it's been used for hundreds of years. I think that sometimes the scientific community has been 'brainwashed' into thinking that everything has to have a scientific explanation! D Boneham

The point I am making and illustrating from the above list is that the general public has no difficulty in accepting the validity of the term 'brainwashing,' and no problem in defining it. In addition, it would be fair to say that all of the above responses would equally apply to people's perception of the word indoctrination.

Freedom from indoctrination and brainwashing.

The journey to freedom is an honest realisation and admittance by oneself that 'I have been indoctrinated or brainwashed.' However, what if a person doesn't know it?

The following is a set of questions which can help reveal if you are being indoctrinated or brainwashed. This is not a test. This is subject only to how honest you want to be about yourself and your life. It is solely between you and you. No one is looking. Be ruthlessly honest if you want to be.

See how many of these questions you can answer with a yes. Never mind what people have told you. What is your heart really saying? Read the following carefully:

1. Are there people in this world today who are indoctrinated or brainwashed about their belief system?

2. Is it possible for people of any age to be indoctrinated or brainwashed without realising it?

3. Is it likely that what indoctrinated or brainwashed people believe, appears so obviously right to them that they feel no need to challenge it?

4. Though a belief system may have been getting reinforced for decades, is it true to say that the reinforcing doesn't make it necessarily true?

5. Is it possible that fear of consequences of having an indoctrinated

or brainwashed faulty belief system, can cause people to avoid ever questioning themselves?

6.   Is it possible that the fear, embarrassment and personal pride can block people from 'hearing' any alternative viewpoint?

7.   Is it possible for large groups of people to all have the same belief but it is a wrong belief?

8.   Is there any possibility whatsoever that you could be indoctrinated or brainwashed right now?

If you have said yes to any of these eight statements, this shows that you believe that indoctrination and brainwashing exists and that it could even apply to you. If you said no to any of the statements it could be because a subconscious belief is being challenged.

Now, taking your strongest religious or political perspective, consider the following questions.

1.   Have you ever asked yourself whether what you believe could be error?

2.   Have you always felt it unnecessary to question your belief because you 'know' it is right?

3.   Have you ever studied what the critics say about your belief?

4.   Can you easily go there now in your mind and explore how it could be error, or do you find that you automatically choose not to go there?

5.   Are there any consequences of changing your belief that would be a disincentive to you?

6.   Would the fear of being wrong for the many years you may have held this belief, keep you from examining your belief too deeply?

7.   If you realised your belief was error and spoke out against it, would likeminded people who you know personally distance themselves from you?

8.   Who told you your belief was the truth? Another person, yourself, some other source?

As you answered these questions did you see a pattern forming? Did you realise something that you may not have thought about before? Did these questions make you feel a little uncomfortable? Being ruthlessly honest with yourself. Have you followed the opinion and teaching of another person more than your own personal discoveries?

The only person that can tell you that you are indoctrinated or brainwashed is yourself. You have a free will to choose what you want to believe and what direction that belief takes you in your life. When we each take responsibility for ourselves and not just follow another blindly like sheep, that is when we can start to be real, be ourselves, be authentic and live true to our self.

My Personal Conclusion

I have devoted a chapter to indoctrination and brainwashing because I want to create awareness of what goes on in many religious groups today. This controlling behaviour towards fellow humans ranges from mild to extreme. How much control is acceptable I ask? We can only answer that from our own perspectives.

I want to expose what I believe happened to me with a view to giving readers an opportunity to really examine themselves, to see if by any chance, their free will has been or is being controlled and therefore violated by another.

In what I'm about to describe, I don't think I've ever been this explicit before, but in the cold light of day, I've searched my soul and answered the simple question; what was it really like?

Here goes.

From my perspective I feel I was 'raped and buggered' by the EB system, not physically, but in my soul. I was overpowered and wilfully controlled by one stronger than me. I was young, vulnerable and weak and innocently gave in to the inflamed desires of the man and the system that gave no concern for my free will and my personal choices.

In effect, this man and system got self-righteous pleasure from my unquestioning submission and their entrance into my soul. I couldn't see what they were doing as it was done from behind, controlled for most of those first 22 years by one man from Neche, North Dakota, who never met me. I was metaphorically shafted with utter contempt and disregard to what I may have wanted. It started as soon as I was born and the coercion, in effect, groomed me to conform to the system. As I grew into my teens and my understanding developed, the soul rape continued, rammed home by eleven, later ten, meetings a week. Awful fearful consequences were introduced to me of losing my Dad and Mum and brothers and the only people I knew, eternal torment in hell, and a life of total failure and deception if I should pull my trousers up and walk away.

I was coercively indoctrinated. To me, that is mental and spiritual abuse. Let me describe what it felt like.

At the time it felt normal, as normal as brushing your teeth twice a day. It felt secure. I was surrounded literally daily, eleven meetings a week with sincere people, people who smiled and lived comfortably and were non-violent. On the surface, all worked hard and most were intelligent and generally well off.

For me, it was all I knew because I was born into the EB belief system. It is one thing to have a belief system changed through brainwashing later in life, but when you are born into a belief system where you don't know any different, then you have no reference to compare with. Like a sitting duck, you are defenceless and vulnerable.

I fully understand that what you have just read may cause offence to some and be considered sensationalist. That is not my intention. As I mentioned before, I am no longer speaking from a wounded or angry place, but from a place where I have a genuine desire to universally expose, what has gone on in the past and what goes on today in many religious cults. It might just help someone.

CHAPTER 17

Coercive Control - Serious Crime Act

how much control is acceptable?

First of all, what a negative subject to write about! Why did feel the need to examine such a sensitive subject and maybe trawl up issues from my past?

Here is why.

I want to draw attention to the fact that coercive control goes on in today's society and at last has been recognised by the government for what it is. I care about those people who have been, and are victims today of this unacceptable infringement. Human life is precious and if you are in any religious organisation, I invite you to examine whether coercive control is happening to members in your group, influenced by the laws that you may be imposing on your members, or laws that your religion might be imposing on you.

Coercive control in an intimate or family relationship became a crime under the Serious Crime Act in 2015. It applies in England and Wales. There are other similar laws in several European countries and in Australia. It applies when one member of a family exerts coercive or controlling behaviour over another member who is aged 16 or over. This is defined as ongoing psychological behaviour, rather than isolated or unconnected incidents, with the purpose of removing a victim's freedom.

The legislation is designed to 'Help victims identify the behaviour they are suffering as wrong and encourage them to report it, [as well as] cause perpetrators to rethink their controlling behaviour.'

According to the official Statutory Guidance, the controlling behaviour of the perpetrator can include:

1. Isolating a person from their friends and family.
2. Monitoring their time.
3. Monitoring a person via online communication tools or using spyware.
4. Taking control over aspects of their everyday life, such as where they can go, who they can see, what to wear and when they can sleep.
5. Depriving them access to support services, such as specialist support or medical services.
6. Repeatedly putting them down such as telling them they are worthless.
7. Control ability to go to school or place of study.
8. Preventing a person from having access to transport or from working.
9. Preventing a person from being able to attend school, college or University.
10. Limiting access to family, friends and finances.

So, was I coercively controlled when I was in the Exclusive Brethren? I shall state facts using the above list as a reference. How they applied to me is just my opinion, I shall let you decide if I was coercively controlled or not.

1. Isolating a person from their friends and family
   From the age of four to twenty-two, I was not allowed to have any contact with any of my four grandparents, two Uncles and Aunts, and ten cousins. When they tried to make contact, they were denied it and not let in the house. I was never allowed to go in the houses of my school friends, and they were never once allowed in our house to play, or for birthday parties or sleepovers. After leaving school I was not allowed to socialise, eat or drink with work colleagues or friends.
2. Monitoring their time
   I had to attend every meeting for 22 years, unless ill. For most of

the time, this was eleven meetings a week, latterly just ten. I had to be at five meetings on a Sunday starting at 6 am, four in the week at 7.45 pm, one at 7.15 pm and Saturday mornings at either 6 am or 10 am. It was not just an expectation, it was EB law. If I stopped going, I could lose my family and friends. Was my time being indirectly monitored?

3. Monitoring a person via online communication tools or using spyware

Computers and mobile phones were strictly forbidden when I was a member, so this did not apply.

4. Taking control over aspects of their everyday life, such as where they can go, who they can see, what to wear and when they can sleep.

The then law, as laid down by the Man of God controlled the type of house we were allowed to live in, the type of drains the house had to have, the jobs we could or could not do, where we could eat, where we could sleep, who we could marry, the length of our hair, the forbidding of pets, the total ban on mobile phones, computers, TV, radio or even anything radio controlled.

We were instructed as to what education or vocations we could not take part in, places we were not allowed to go to like cinema, theatre, sporting events or theme parks, which relatives we had to be isolated from, and the limiting of access to people, for example school friends or anyone outside the EB. Sharing a meal with literally anyone who wasn't an EB member, even having a cup of tea with such a neighbour, was a 'wicked sin.' We all knew too well that any coming out from under the control would mean being cut off, maybe for life, from our family and friends if they should stay in.

5. Depriving them access to support services, such as specialist support or medical services.

I remember psychologists, counsellors and the like being strongly discouraged but I don't know to what extent.

6. Repeatedly putting them down such as telling them they are worthless.

Whilst growing up, I was being told that we were in the only 'right' position on earth and knowing no different, I totally believed it. The implication of this to me was that everyone else was worthless.

7. Control ability to go to school or place of study.

After I was sixteen, I knew that if I went to University it would mean being cut off completely from my family, maybe for life. I could have got an apprenticeship at a photographer's that I was interested in but because it involved working Saturdays, I was told I could not work there.

8.   Preventing a person from having access to transport or from working.

I was allowed to work but only in certain types of jobs. As I mentioned in the previous point, I was not allowed to work Saturdays, so I gave up the possibility of pursuing a career and a passion in photography because of the fear of the consequences.

9.   Preventing a person from being able to attend school, college or University.

University was forbidden.

10.   Limiting access to family, friends and finances.

(As in number 1)

Conclusion.

What do you do if you believe that God is telling you to be separate from your family and community, which in effect, kills your family unit? You are probably aware that in some parts of the world, some people believe their god is instructing them to literally kill people who are not aligned to their beliefs.

Herein lies a problem. Many religious fundamental cults are sincerely following what their Leader says their god is instructing them to do. Their intents are not because they necessarily hate people. It is because they are indoctrinated or brainwashed into stealing people's happiness, killing innocent men, women and children, and destroying humanity. Leaders of such groups impose their laws on their gullible followers that classify 'the enemy' as evil, resulting in shunning, separating and splitting families and marriages, sometimes killing them, then denying all responsibility!

In effect, they are saying, 'They were the 'evil' ones. It's not our fault. We are not a cult. We are the right church or religion. We follow God and the other 39,999 religious organisations don't follow God.'

They all have one thing in common. They all believe that through their leader, it is God himself who is instructing them to behave in these ways.

In effect, this is what virtually every one of these religions/organisations/cults are saying.

SHAKE IT ALL ABOUT

You might be forgiven for thinking, what a shambles! How shallow and almost primitive to have this arrogance and self –importance, yet it is what can happen when mankind gravitates to his vain judgements of what he deems good and evil.

When a religion offers the sniff of meeting basic human needs, the need to feel safe, the powerful need for belonging, the intoxicating feeling of having self-esteem, the lure of actualising through being aligned to 'God' himself, it can cause people to throw themselves into whatever their religion tells them their 'God' is saying.

So how can decent intelligent humans get to the place whereby their minds and wills are taken over by a coercively controlling person or system? Well, they most certainly can and here are some of the main factors that cause such a state:

1.   Fear of the consequences of believing something different. For example, if a person believes that if they were to believe contrary to what they have been taught, could result in the separation of their husband/wife/children/home or business, then this can be a powerful disincentive from even considering an alternative viewpoint.
2.   Fear of having been wrong for maybe many decades. The thought that decades of life have been lived in a terrible error and waste can be enough to avoid all thought connected to any alternative.
3.   Immersing themselves only with people who believe the same thing. Spending lots of time with people who believe the same as you helps to reinforce beliefs, strengthen them, and eliminate possibilities of the belief being error.
4.   Pride and ego rising up to protect their 'rightness.' The pride of man and his ego does not like being wrong at the best of times and when so much is at stake, the sting of having to even admit that they have been wrong can prevent people from even looking at any alternative viewpoint.

When you get these four traits running in the mind of a person, and there are other traits too, then this is how an indoctrinated and coercively controlled person reacts to suggestions contrary to his / her beliefs. Though their ears hear the suggestion, they literally block the thought from getting into their mind. Like a stopcock on a toilet, a valve shuts and closes down this 'enemy thought' that violates what the person believes. Like putting your hands over your ears and making a noise so you can't hear what someone is saying, the mind of a coercively controlled person refuses access to anything that threatens their belief system. They simply do not 'hear' anything contrary to what they want to believe.

This was my personal experience with being reared in the Exclusive Brethren. We had the 'truth,' the Universal Leader, the correct bible translation and interpretation. I was taught that everything outside our enclosed exclusive walls was worldly and of the devil. Why would I even want to listen to anything contrary?

Now in fairness, such people are exercising their free will to not 'hear' anything contrary. That is their choice. However, it becomes a problem in society when these same people start to coerce others by taking away their free will and controlling it through laws and rules with dire consequences should they disobey.

Such groups/cults might well by default, have family or household members that contravene the above Serious Crime Act 2015 and coercively control their members. Every group is different. Religious control in most groups ranges somewhere between 0 and 100%.

Many only exert a small amount of control, for example by giving off vibes of displeasure if you miss some of their meetings. At the other end of the scale are the cults that control the members' lives in every way to the point that when they call for mass suicide, the members obey without question.

We saw this in 1978 when the brainwashed followers in the People's Temple in Jonestown were ordered by their leader to poison themselves. 909 followers including 276 children died in the space of a few hours.

In 1994 the New Age leader of The Order of the Solar Temple cult brainwashed 74 of his followers into committing suicide. He told them it was necessary to enter a higher spiritual plane.

In 1997 the Heaven's Gate cult followed their leader and 39 committed suicide believing his instructions to reach an extra-terrestrial spacecraft that was following a comet.

Let me ask you a question. What level of control is acceptable to you? I believe that is for you and me to decide individually. For me only zero control is acceptable. True leadership never controls, it only ever serves, respects, facilitates, empowers and releases people to achieve for themselves and others.

So, what if you have come to realise that you are under the control of a leader that you follow? I suggest there are three possibilities to consider.

1.   If you like the control and want to continue following your leader then carry on.

2.   If you don't like being controlled but choose to not rock the boat, then carry on and live with a conflict of values you will inevitably be experiencing.

3.   Seek out help and leave. (See chapter on How to leave the cult you are in).

If you feel you have been coercively controlled and would like to know more, check out the following website:

https://www.sanctuarycriminaljustice.com/

CHAPTER 18

My gratitude to my parents.

Some parents go by the Bible verse that says, 'train up a child in the way he should go, and when he grows old, he shall not depart from it.'

The question with that is, 'WHAT IS, the way the child should go?'

Many parents bring up their children their way; their religion, their beliefs, their traditions, their denominations, their chosen path, in the hope their children will stay on their path.

Have you ever known Christian parents to bring their children up as a Muslim? Muslim parents to bring up their children as Jews? Jewish parents to bring up their children as Christians?

So, my parent's intention, in keeping with their tradition, was to train their four boys up to follow God through the Christian religion. However, if we are going to be accurate and literal about this, they trained their four boys to follow God through Christianity, according to the teaching of their 'Man of God'. Like many parents, they were 100% sincere and totally believed their way was the right way, the best way, the only way. Sound familiar?

After 50 years of seeing the fruit of the way of the EB, I can now see clearly that I was brought up in a religion of law, conditions, rules and regulations.

However, there were some very good aspects of my upbringing which I am grateful for and I want to honour my parents in this chapter.

My parents loved each other and as Dad once said, "We are one." I never heard a negative word spoken between them. They never even raised their voices towards each other ever. They both gave each other 100%. Their marriage commitment was total and devoid of any distance or separation or upset. Dad lived his role as the man, the husband and the father, while mum lived her part as the woman, wife and mother. They were an inseparable team both supporting and submitting to each other's roles. Their values were identical.

In bringing us four boys up, they did their best with what they knew and what they had. Dad worked extremely hard in successfully providing for his family, despite the adversity he faced, walking in beautiful humility and compassion. Mum worked extremely hard in bringing four boys up. Mum was one of the best cooks in the world and they both shared the gift of hospitality.

Dad went on his own to the Pier Head in Liverpool in his lunchtimes for 20 years telling people about Jesus. He didn't let anyone knowing he was doing this because he wasn't doing it for recognition. Both were totally sincere and dedicated to the family. They sowed the seed in us that Jesus Christ is the Son of God. For that, I am eternally grateful.

I experienced community and saw how this can be a support, help stability, and in certain ways, it can affirm a person growing up. However, when it produces self-righteousness, narrow-mindedness and a 'them and us' mentality, it causes segregation, selfishness and isolation from all mankind.

One of the best aspects of the EB was that marriage was seen as sacred and for life. Divorce was not a mindset that we had. One divorce in 50 years shows this. This is better than the normalising of marital strife and divorce that is so prevalent in society today.

I enjoyed fantastic food from talented home cooking. The older women taught the younger women culinary skills and with the continual hospitality in each other's houses, it meant they were all well-practised and the standard was extremely high. Most restaurant food comes nowhere near the quality I experienced but nowadays I love having the freedom to eat out if I want to.

I appreciated the manners, respect, decency and kindness of the culture. People under strict religious law often conform to such codes and conventions. Nowadays though, I also enjoy the raw honesty and expression of many people, not all cultured and honed but real, genuine, and down to earth.

I appreciated the work ethic and attitude to providing for the family. This is an advantage of community where people can get advice and support from those who have your interest at heart.

Thank you, Dad and Mum. You are the best.
Love John.

CHAPTER 19

Letter to My Old Friends

let's talk

Dear old friends, who are still members of the Exclusive Brethren aka Plymouth Brethren Christian Church,

Hello, how are you all? I'm John Spinks. Some of you will remember me from the Liverpool assembly a good few years ago. Hi Max, Tomo, Ian Co, my old best friends. Some of you will know my Dad, the greatest pourer of Scotch, and my dear Mum, best cakes on the planet; great parents. So, it's been a while since we used to have a good few laughs, 1988 in fact. I disappeared all of a sudden if you remember. You must have been devastated ⍰

Anyway, why am I writing to you now, and why should you even read something from someone who is very, very misbehaved according to certain laws?

By the way, you don't have to read this letter if you don't want to. You are free as far as I'm concerned. If you keep on reading, you'll find that I'm just going to be real with you, honest and to the point, well, I might ramble a little. Some things haven't changed!

You see, I've grown up a little from my youthful years, quite a lot in fact. I seem to have a lot more love nowadays, that's what I mean by growing up. Love is the only measure of worth, the only currency of value and the only hope for mankind, well that's what I've come to experience anyway. Does that sound good to you? I mean, God is love, can't get any higher than love, can we? And, I love you too. I really do, I feel love for you in my heart, it's there, and I reckon you love me too. There's a good reason to communicate don't you think?

First of all, I want you to know that I am not aiming to violate your free will. Love never does this. I have no desire to disturb your trajectory in your life and change you. You are free to follow any doctrine or man that you want to. You have your life journey to explore your heart and make the decisions that you choose. You ought to be loved no matter what and given the space to make up your own mind. I will not violate the space you choose to be in. That would be control and presumption.

I am not being presumptuous when I say that I know how you feel. My heart had a 'bent', an aptitude from my upbringing like you have. I knew nothing else. You don't either. I know the lens that you are looking through right now. I was 4th generation Exclusive Brethren like many of you are. I was born into it. I grew up in it. I was immersed in it and my only reference in my life was this one lens. I saw everything through this one lens. Everything was filtered through this one lens. Let us be honest. I wasn't encouraged or allowed to have another lens, and neither are you. I saw and you see everything through the lens of the person that you call The Man of God. Maybe you have never really considered that. I remember that feeling and that lens well.

How do I see that lens nowadays? In a way, I don't really want to tell you. I love and accept you as you are unconditionally. I don't require you to change your lens to change my love, attitude and stance towards you. However, I do want to tell you about a love that I never dreamed was possible or true. It is perfect love, which is not perfect according to man's experience and interpretations. This love confounds the wise. This love is way off the scale of man's knowledge of good and evil interpretations of love. I have come to know this perfect love in a way that can best be described as unconditional love. This is where you are loved without any conditions required on your part and where you are loved no matter what condition you are in, unconditionally.

This perfect unconditional love does not have terms and conditions, stipulations, requirements, demands, obligations, prerequisites, boundaries, time-scales or laws to obey. To receive it, you just have to believe. No, not believe to get it, but believe to realise that it is and was already there, waiting patiently for you to open your door and allow it in. This is because this perfect unconditional

love will not violate your will. It will not push your door down and force its way in. It will not roll its eyes in frustration and get annoyed with you when you refuse to accept its gentle knock on your door. It will not threaten to punish, hurt, or destroy you. There is no fear in this love, absolutely no fear whatsoever, not one iota of fear in fact. There is nothing to be scared of. There is no fear that one day this love will lose patience with you. There is no fear that it will ever run out of time. This is because it is eternal, it lasts forever, it never gives up, it never changes, and it never changes its unconditional nature. It never eventually introduces conditions. It never puts you under the remotest form of pressure to conform or obey. It does say follow but only in the meekest, humblest, gentlest of ways, so gentle, just like a still small voice, that if you are making a noise you might not even hear it.

If man is making a big noise in your life by putting pressure on you, telling you that you are under law, giving you conditions to meet, placing boundaries around your life, expecting you to meet certain requirements, any requirements, tying you into terms and conditions, controlling any aspect of your lifestyle via rules, commanding you to follow him, teaching you that your identity is determined by your level of conformity to his latest dictates, demanding unswerving loyalty to whatever he tells you to believe.....

.....then you are unlikely to hear the still, small, ever so gentle voice. This is the voice of perfect unconditional love that will just keep you in his heart, hold you in his affections, maintain steadfast hope and faith in you, and will wait and wait until the day you realise that the noise of rules, regulations, laws, conditions and expectations were never ever going to transform you into realising that you are a Love Child of God. They were only capable of enslaving you, dividing you, ostracising you, prosecuting you, condemning you, separating you, self-righteousfying you and eventually killing you. When you see the end, and I mean the very end of man's noise, then with great relief and abandon, you give in and give up your attempts to conform to man. You will then realise that there is nowhere else to go but into the eternal arms of perfect unconditional love. Love that is for you, not against you. Love that died for his enemies, a love that casts out all fear, a perfect love that never fails. Unconditional Love is a person. Not a person who evolves and changes laws for you and demands your obedience or else! No, the person I am referring to is the same yesterday, today and forever. Do you know him?

So dear Brother or Sister, which includes all mankind, He is why I write this letter to you. I only have one message for you. Don't follow man. Follow Him. Peace to you all.

Love John

CHAPTER 20

The Ghosts of Allerton Road.

What I am about to share may appear far-fetched and for that reason I considered leaving it out. There are some stories people just do not tell for many reasons. Well, I'm not going to fear what people may think who read this one. On balance, it is probably just as unbelievable as 45,000 plus sensible people, calling a drain pipe 'worldly.' All I will say, though extraordinary, is that this is what literally happened with no exaggeration. As for the conclusion, I will give my thoughts about it at the end and leave it for you to think about yourself if you want to. If this subject is not one you want to read about then skip this chapter.

Phil, I'm using a different name, was born in Liverpool, of a similar age, and three years a friend through our work. A large group of us worked in sales and promotion and we socialised together with pool, snooker, many evenings in pubs and bars talking football, music, women, putting the world to right and finishing off with a Chinese or an Indian meal.

Phil and I both shared a love for Queen the rock band and we would often go for a drive listening to Queens Greatest Hits I and II on the cassette tape player in the car playing full blast.

It is 17th December 1995. This is the third Sunday evening this month that Phil and I have visited a night club called Reds on Edge Lane in Liverpool. We went about 11 o'clock just for a quiet drink. Being a Sunday, Reds closed at midnight. Afterwards, we went driving around Liverpool for a couple of hours enjoying Freddie, Brian, John and Roger with their We Are the Champions, I Want to Break Free, It's a Hard Life, The Show Must Go On etc.

On this night I asked Phil if he would like us to drive to some known haunted locations around Liverpool. We had experienced some horrific times earlier on in the year with manifestations of some very disturbing 'spirits,' but evidently, I had not learnt the lesson which was to 'avoid all that stuff.'

I want to point out that on this night, I had only one pint of lager, Phil two at the most, and both of us had never taken drugs in our life.

It has just gone midnight. The roads are quiet. The temperature is close to freezing. We drive a few miles to Allerton Road, where the main Liverpool EB meeting room which holds about 600 people is situated. I stop outside the entrance which are metal barred gates that are closed and padlocked. From the car we peer into the darkness through the gates. Suddenly we both become aware of a disturbing presence coming towards us rapidly from behind the gates. With it came an increasing vile odour that we both agree afterwards smelt like death. As it gets closer the fear causes me to let the clutch out and drive off.

We drive down to Mather Avenue and take the left fork towards Springwood cemetery where some of my ancestors are buried. Just before the traffic lights at Woolton Road, I switch the engine off and we talk about what we have just experienced. As we are talking, I suddenly see Phil's jaw drop and he is staring past me through the driver's window. "What are you looking at?" I immediately ask. "That old lady tapping on the window," he replied staring wide eyed. Then his eyes went to the back of the car and he said, "She's gone through the back door and she's sitting behind you now." I couldn't see anything, but I felt a presence behind me. I turned around to touch her and Phil said that he saw my hand go right through her body. She disappeared. We drive past the cemetery and take a left turn into Hillfoot Road. After about a hundred yards Phil started to choke as if he was about to vomit. I slammed the brakes on, but Phil said, 'keep going' and after a few seconds he felt fine. It seemed that the location he choked at had a cold presence so at the traffic lights I did a U turn and we drive back down Hillfoot Road which is a duel carriageway. As we approach the same location Phil starts to choke again and this time we stop, and Phil gets out. I look to my right and on a tree in the middle of the carriageway there are flowers placed there. It looks as though someone had recently died.

We turn around again and drive to Woolton Village where I know of another so-called haunted place. We turn into Church Road and fifty yards up by a sandstone gate post Phil sees a man in a monk's brown habit. We stop and Phil gets out of the car. I watched him walk to the gate post, turn around and get back into the car. He told me that he had walked into the monk who disappeared as soon as Phil touched him. Why did Phil want to do that? I don't know but we were fascinated, exhilarated, scared and enchanted by this supernatural phenomenon. We now drive up the road where a long sandstone wall has a Catholic convent behind it. It was here seven years previously that a friend with me had seen a cream coloured nun here, dressed in old fashioned apparel, shimmering and standing by the wall.

So, to continue the story, here we are approaching that sandstone wall and as we do, we are both electrified with goose pimples. I stop at the end of the wall at the junction of Church Road and Beaconsfield Road. Here there are large iron gates and behind them a park and the grounds of the convent. We stand in front of these gates and look through. Phil pointed to what he could see and described a nun shimmering, cream colour. She was hanging in a tree about fifty yards away. He was describing exactly what my friend had seen seven years previously just along the road.

Then within seconds, Phil is telling me that the nun has moved and is now standing the other side of the gate about six feet away from us. Though I could not see what Phil was seeing, I could tangibly feel what were like strong waves of penetrating cold. I was feeling rather terrified, fascinated, and tingling all over. From deep within me I speak out these words that just instantly come to me. 'Lord Jesus, have mercy on this soul.' Immediately Phil saw the nun shoot back through the trees and disappear. We drive down Beaconsfield Road, past Strawberry Field, where nothing is real, but this is, (couldn't resist that one), take a left down Menlove Avenue and round a few corners back to Allerton Road from the opposite direction to before. All this time we have been talking, trying to comprehend these manifestations and asking each other, can we handle it or shall we go back home. We should have gone back home.

I drive up to the same gates of the EB meeting room as before. I leave the engine running, foot on the brake, shaken with fear yet so exhilarated by the past hour or so. What happened next was the most frightening thing I've ever experienced. We both experienced a strong presence and a vile smell of death rushing up the drive again from behind the gates. Then suddenly Phil points out of his window and said in a strained voice, "See that?" "See what?" I asked. Phil described about 20 men and women standing there looking at us from behind the gates. The men had long dark coats and were wearing trilby hats. The women wore hats and long dresses and sounded just like Brethren of old in the old photographs that I had seen in family albums growing up. Phil of course had never seen such photographs. Phil said they were all looking very sombre and were all staring at us. In the centre was a tall man with a small woman. The goose pimple feeling and fear was so strong and I remember asking Phil repeatedly, 'Can you take this, shall we go, are you ok?' Phil was asking me the same questions. Then Phil said they were now on our side of the gate and now had started to surround the car. His passenger window was 8 inches down and suddenly I witnessed Phil's left arm being, what looked like being, yanked through the window and as if someone was tugging it violently. His body was pulled up against the door and if the door had been opened, he would have shot out of the car. Phil was screaming.

This all happened in the space of a few seconds and simultaneously I felt my body being lifted up off my seat, so my head banged on the car ceiling. As Phil told me they were surrounding the car, I had subconsciously put the car in first gear with the clutch in and the handbrake off. As I felt my body being lifted up, I stamped on the accelerator and released the clutch causing the tyres to screech as we sped off down Allerton Road.

Within a few seconds Phil's body slumped down as if he was unconscious or dead even. I was absolutely terrified. If he is dead, it is all my fault I remember thinking. He didn't know Jesus, he was unprotected, what shall I do? I knew exactly what I was going to do.

I was going straight to the Police Station at the end of Allerton Road opposite Allerton library. I was going to march up to the desk and tell them that a spirit had tried to pull my friend out of the car through the window. In these minutes of extreme fear and panic I was not thinking entirely rationally, yet I had the wherewithal to know that the police would breathalyse me and not believe me. I didn't care if they arrested me. I wanted human company. I had been spending the last hour or so in the weird realm of weird spirits, if that's what they were, and I wanted some human normality and sense. Phil was dead for all I knew. This was not a humorous moment. The reason I say that is because of what happened next.

To my horror the Police Station had gone part time and was closed. I parked outside under a street light. As I stopped the car Phil sat up suddenly and looked at me. He was laughing, a sort of mocking laugh and staring at me in a focused sort of way. Now I enjoy having a laugh, I like jokes and being silly, but I can tell you, this was not the time for humour. This was out-of-the-box terrifying. So, I said to him, "What are you laughing at Phil?"

"You are soft, you should not have left where we have just come from," was his strange reply. Phil had never used the word 'soft' and afterwards admitted it was a word he never used. However, I remember my great aunt Irene used to use it. She had been a member of the EB. Then, as if a strong person had hold of him by the lapels, Phil was thrown backwards and forwards from the seat to the windscreen at a speed that was not humanly possible. After about half a minute he slumped down again as if he was unconscious.

I was going to the next Police Station. This was not a dream. This was actually happening. I was terrified. On the way I passed a garage on Smithdown Road. The bright lights and the human cashier drew me there plus I was thirsty after all that freakiness. As I stopped the car Phil who appeared unconscious sat bolt upright again and said these exact words to me. "John, do you want to see something scary?" "No I don't," I replied instantly. "John, do you want to see something really scary?" "No I do not," I snapped back. "John, do you want to see something really, really scary?" he asked the third time. I was looking away as soon as he had asked this question the first time. "No, shut up, I do not want to," I said and got out the car to get two drinks.

I drove off heading for the Police Station a mile away on Wavertree Road. On the way we passed Smithdown Road cemetery. As we passed the gates Phil started getting thrown violently back and forwards again. With my left hand I tried to hold him away from the steering wheel as I tried to keep the car on the road with my right hand. We got to the Police Station by which time Phil had slumped down again.

I ran into the Police Station. It was 2 o'clock Monday morning. I could not see any one on the desk but before I got there, I saw a pay phone in the foyer. I changed my mind about telling the Police and phoned a friend who I thought might be able to help me. I woke this friend up and told him what had been happening. Half asleep, he just said that Phil had become demon possessed and was not good company to be around. If he didn't get saved, he could end up in a psychiatric home or commit suicide. He told me to stand in faith and not budge. Though that wasn't a lot of practical help to me I got back in the car. Phil was sitting up. "What happened?" I ask him.

SHAKE IT ALL ABOUT

Speaking quite normally he told me that an old woman back at Allerton Road had grabbed his arm, tried to pull him out of the car and had entered him.

What would you have done?

I still felt responsible for taking Phil to those haunted places and I didn't want him going home on his own and maybe taking his life. These are the thoughts that went through my head. So, I decided to take him back to my flat in Lisburn Lane, Tuebrook, Liverpool where he stayed for a week.

That is the end of the story for now, as far as the incident at the EB's meeting room at Allerton Road is concerned.

However, now I've told you this much, I guess you would like to know what happened to Phil. That terrifying night, especially between midnight and 2am, wasn't the end of the story by any means and I don't feel happy leaving it at that horrible stage. Do remember, this is all what literally happened.

For a week Phil manifested what some would describe as demon possession. Deep guttural voices which weren't his would come out of him, swearing, accusing and threatening. This was not like Phil. Our friendship was respectful with never a bad word said between us. Something had happened to him. Maybe it was that old woman who came through the gates in Allerton Road. What else could it be? Cutting the long story short, the following Saturday and Sunday, which was New Year's Eve, Phil had a 17-hour sleep. Usually he only ever slept three to four hours every night as he had a very unusual metabolism. After he woke at 9am on that Sunday morning he called me and told me to call round immediately.

Fearing a possible scary manifestation, I first called round to pick up a good friend called Ronnie. I sure wasn't going to go on my own. We turned up at Phil's front door at 10am and he ushered us inside. 'You won't believe what has happened,' he said. I fell asleep at 4 o'clock yesterday afternoon and only woke an hour ago. Phil then described a vision he had whilst asleep. He had never read a Bible in his life so as he told us the vision we were amazed as he described the book of Revelation in great detail that he had seen happening in front of him. After that vision a man in white had appeared to Phil saying, 'I am the Root of David.' For 20 minutes Phil recounted what the man had told him, and Ronnie and I listened wide eyed because Phil was quoting texts from the Bible that he had never heard. At the end the man in white said to him that this very night, Phil would be baptised in water in his name, and that he would then baptise him with his Holy Spirit.

What happened that night was that Phil was invited to a New Year's Eve celebration in 31 Stoneby Drive, Wallasey with a group of Christians. Just before midnight he was baptised in a full bath in the name of the Father, Son, and Holy Spirit. As he came up out of the water he started speaking in tongues and was filled with great joy. Phil's life was instantly transformed. The vexation, torment and bad voices stopped instantly, and Phil's life was filled with love, joy and peace. For the next seven weeks he stayed at mine sleeping on the sofa. Seven supernatural events took place during this time. It would take another book to describe them all.

So, has this story been profitable or significant? Here are some questions that I have had that maybe only time will reveal what the answers might be.

What do those twenty 'spirits' and that vile smell of death that were behind the EB meeting room gates signify?

Why did they surround the car?

Why did the old woman, who was a spirit try to physically pull Phil out of the car?

Why, after the woman entered Phil, did he say to me that 'I was soft, I shouldn't have left where we had just come from?'

I include this story not to make a point because I can't prove anything from it. I rather suspect it is a manifestation of deep-rooted, hard-core religious legalism. I'll let you come to your own conclusions.

One thing I am sure about. I am very grateful for the man in white who visited Phil. The result of that was plain enough for all of us to see.

CHAPTER 21

So, what is a Religious Cult?

let's examine the facts

You cannot call a book Cult Escape without explaining the significance of the word 'cult' and defining exactly what you mean by it. The group I escaped from deny that they were a cult. On top of that, many academics cannot even agree what a cult is. Then there are cult apologists, cult defenders, cult sympathizers, anti-cult and counter-cult movements, who come from sociological and/or theological angles, and whom all tend to disagree with one another.

The challenge in defining whether a group is a religious cult or not is that groups with cultic hallmarks or tendencies vary in the intensity of control, from very mild to hardcore. A question therefore could be asked: Where do you draw the line about what is or is not a cult? How controlling does a group have to be for it to be considered a cult? It seems to me that this is what academics cannot agree on and therefore they fail to agree on what a cult is.

There is definitely the spectrum of intensity of control in many religious groups. However, for clarity and for the purposes of Cult Escape, I am referring primarily to groups that are so utterly devoted to their leader, so strict in their cultic laws and families are so clearly divided by these laws, that it is obvious that they are a cult. As to how much control you deem is acceptable, that is a question only you can decide.

So, this chapter seeks to give a fair and balanced examination of what a cult is, by exploring the following questions and factors:

1.   Definitions of the word 'cult.'
2.   What is the public perception about what a cult is?
3.   How can you tell if a religious group is a cult or not?
4.   Twelve cult-related questions to consider.
5.   Were the Exclusive Brethren that I was born into a cult?
6.   Is the rebranded Plymouth Brethren Christian Church (PBCC), a cult today?

Definitions of the word 'cult.'

English Oxford Dictionaries define 'cult' simply as a 'system of religious veneration and devotion directed towards a particular figure or object.'

The Merriam Webster Dictionary defines it even simpler as 'a system of religious beliefs and ritual.'

Webster's 1913 Dictionary goes a bit further and defines it as a system of intense religious veneration of a particular person, idea, or object, especially one considered spurious or irrational to traditional religious bodies; as, the Moonie cult.

The Christian Research Institute begins to unpack these definitions by saying that a cult is a religious or semi-religious sect whose members are controlled almost entirely by a single individual or by an organization. This kind of cult is usually manipulative, demanding total commitment and loyalty from its followers. Converts are usually cut off from all former associations, including their own families.

An article in christianitytoday.com describes the most commonly used definition of a cult as:

1) Exclusive. They may say, "We are the only ones with the truth; everyone else is wrong, and if you leave our group your salvation is in danger."

2) Secretive. Certain teachings are not available to outsiders or they're presented only to certain members, sometimes after taking vows of confidentiality.

3) Authoritarian. A human leader expects total loyalty and unquestioned obedience.

There appears to be little consensus in defining what a cult is. If we are looking for an academically scientific definition, we probably won't find it. I suggest that to understand the word we have to examine the similarities in dictionary definitions, similarities in reports of ex-members and media reports, compare obvious hallmarks of cults that have always been labelled as such, and observe the effects such a group has on its followers and ex-followers.

What is the public perception about what a cult is?

If all that isn't enough, consider the perspectives of the following twenty-one random adults, who responded to a survey which asked the question, 'How would you describe what a religious cult is?'

The following are all the comments by people that answered the question. All were asked if they wanted their name or initials included. Some wanted to remain anonymous:

1. Control. Where a leader controls a group of people with their religious beliefs. Graham Robinson

2. Insecure. It's a group of people who do not feel on solid ground with their beliefs, so turn to rules, control and fear tactics to keep the group together, dividing them from people they believe would change their minds, including family and other loved ones. Ian Denny

3. I think a cult is following of people of influence who are manipulating. Samira Ali

4. Sadly what comes to mind for me is a religious group imposing a way of life, often misogynistic and abusive. Mel Riley

5. Control. In my opinion, a cult is any group that uses the fear of punishment as a control factor limiting freedom and liberty. MK

6. A group of people who control others within a flock according to their beliefs and limitations. Rahila Khan

7. Group of people following religious ideals and rules enforced by a figurehead who has total control over the followers. Anon

8. Lack of freedom. If you don't have the choice to leave or are brainwashed as such. Waco, Texas springs to mind. Where people are manipulated into thinking the leader of that group is allowed to do anything to them. Sharon Brown

9. People in those are literally brainwashed and slaves without having the right to have a choice and are manipulated in every way possible. Their reality has been so much crippled they don't know who they are anymore. The truth has to come out in the open for all to see. Ganka Wolbers

10. To me, it means a combination of things: blind zeal, passion, mind

control, megalomania, manipulation, conversion, corruption, abuse of power, brainwashing, charismatic/persuasive but deluded leader. Adults are free to be idiots and choose this. What gets me raging is involving kids. Anon

11. Control. Preying on people who are lacking something emotionally, or who feel they do not fit in at home or in society. Paula Littzen

12. If it's harder to get out than it is to get in, it's a cult. If they try to manipulate, coerce, or threaten an ex-member to keep you from telling the truth, it's a cult. If someone's preferences & individual opinions for living their life (with harm to none) are invalidated or condemned, it's a cult. If they claim to have more authority over a member's life than they actually have a right to, it's a cult. If members of a cult think they have free will, but clearly have been manipulated or brainwashed into thinking they do when they actually don't, it's a cult. If they freak out when someone calls it a cult, it's a cult. Amanda

13. People are either born into cults or easy meat for them because their personal and therefore, home life too, don't make them feel worthy. Never tell your kids what to do, ask them and tell them why you're asking and if they have a valid reason not to do it, respect that. Phil Murphy

14. Where individuals lose their right to think for themselves. Kapil Kapur

15. A grouping of people who are asked by their leader(s) to abandon any form of critical thinking and accept as the only truth their teachings, and where any attempts at debunking these teachings will incur punishment and reprisal. CBW

16. Emotional manipulation of human needs for a predetermined personal end. Sam Dalton

17. Communities or groups with a rigid structure of rules and beliefs that are controlled and reinforced through mind manipulation and harsh punishments for non-conforming members. (((don't know that just came to me))) Murilyn

18. It's a difficult one (no pun intended) I didn't think it had to always be related to religion. My understanding is it is a collective of people that share the same beliefs/thoughts but do not appreciate any challenges from others nor make it easy for people within the collective to leave and by nature are quite isolated from mainstream society. Latoya Maynard

19. A cult is a complex group of people who are driven by the same cause that in their mind is the right and just path. Emma Preston
20. A cult is a restricted and controlled group of people directed to follow a common cause. Anon
21. I don't really know but I would think the presence of a leader, often highly charismatic, who demands complete loyalty and service would be part of any definition. Mark Elgar

When we take all of the above definitions and perspectives into account, I believe we have reached a fair and rational description of what a cult is. If we studied even more dictionary definitions and surveyed another thousand people for their perspectives, I believe we would arrive at the same conclusions.

How can you tell if a religious group is a cult or not?
Using the above dictionary definitions, descriptions and viewpoints, the following is a general checklist which gives clues as to whether a group is a cult or not:

1. The group have extreme and unquestioning commitment to its leader whether he is alive or dead.
2. The group regard their leader's belief system, ideology, rules and regulations as the truth and as law.
3. The leader dictates the lifestyle of the members which may include where they live, how often they will meet, what jobs they can do, what they wear, what schools they go to, what food they eat, what friends they can have, what contact they are allowed to have with people.
4. Laws and rules are made by the leader who usually has no accountability. He is generally a law unto himself.
5. There are official rules, regulations, restrictions and conditions that the followers feel obliged to keep. There are also unspoken rules and expectations which meet with contempt or condemnation if not kept.
6. The group maintains that they are the main ones or the only ones who hold the truth, which creates a polarised us-and-them mentality.
7. The group maintains that any person that is not in agreement with them, is in error.
8. There are unspoken consequences or even threats that if you

leave you could lose contact with family and friends, lose your job, your house, your status etc. Then there are spiritual implications. For example, you are out of God's will or the worst threat being that they say you will go to hell and be tormented forever.

9. The leader demands absolute loyalty and unquestioning commitment. Asking questions is discouraged and punished as it shows signs of mistrust.

10. Members are indoctrinated or brainwashed into believing that there can be no life outside the group. They believe there is no alternative and no need to examine their beliefs because they are 'right.'

Twelve cult-related questions to consider.

Q: Are religious cults really such a significant problem?

A: Independent reported in 1994 that more than 500 cults that use mind control to recruit and keep members, were operating in the United Kingdom and that up to half a million people in Britain are, or have been, involved with a cult.

In 2014, the UK's Cult information Centre stated that there is an estimated 500 to 1000 cults in the UK and that they are on the rise.

Another study noted that a conservative estimate is that between two million and five million Americans have experienced cult participation.

An Australian government committee in 2000 estimated that, while exact numbers of members are unknown, two or three per cent of the population, about 500,000 people, in Australia are involved in cults in one way or another.

An article on The Impact of Cults on Health noted that with this level of involvement, even a low incidence of abuse is likely to mean that thousands of people are affected.

Q: How are some people affected?

A: Apart from my own experiences at the time, and the benefit of hindsight, I have done extensive research into the effects cults have on people. I have chatted to hundreds of ex-members and am in the process of compiling their experiences that will be published on the website www.cult-escape.com I am not exaggerating when I say that many lives have been destroyed, not least by the separation of their loved ones for life. Many have not seen their families for decades and many have missed the marriages of their children and the births of their grandchildren. When a person is coercively indoctrinated into a close-knit 'family' and later is ostracised, shunned and cut off, the effects on that human life can be devastating. One lady told me that she left the EB in 1960 and is still traumatised by her experiences 57 years later. Who cares? Well after having my family split for 48 years to date, I do.

Q: What makes a person join a cult?

A: A variety of reasons such as a need to belong, wanting to be loved and accepted, being vulnerable, wanting a purpose in life, or curious and getting deceived by the lures of esoteric knowledge. Many are in a transition period of their life and are looking for something to put their faith into. Many like myself were born into a cult and grow up thinking it is 'normal.'

Q: What is esoteric knowledge?

A: Esoteric means private; secret; confidential and is intended to be revealed only to the initiates of a group. It is "special knowledge understood by a select few."

Q: What is the 'honeymoon' period in a cult?

A: When a person joins a cult, they are treated very carefully, given great respect, lots of attention, flattery and 'love,' (love bombing) and are made to feel that they truly belong there. This sudden 'feeling very important' can be intoxicating to the unsuspecting victim. By the time full confidence is established, usually around three months, the victim will have been indoctrinated and brainwashed and will now be ready to come under obligations, demands and expectation.

Q: When people join a cult do they realise it is a cult?

A: No. Cults don't advertise themselves as cults. All, in fact, say that they are not a cult.

Q: What are the potential biggest problems for anyone in a cult?

A: The disrespect of your individuality. The control and at worse, the rape of your soul. The telling you how to live your life. The grooming of you into being a clone made in their image. The crushing of your free will and like a bonsai tree, the cutting of your roots so that you never grow into your true potential.

On top of all that, the separating of families which prevents normal family life.

Q: What is soul rape?

A: This is where a person overpowers the soul of another and their egos are gratified by the control over their victim's mind, will and emotions.

Q: What type of person joins a cult?

A: No particular type. Cults can seduce people from every corner of society ranging from those uneducated to those well-educated, from those emotionally unintelligent to those emotionally intelligent and from those with every type of background and upbringing.

Q: Should people be allowed to be in a cult?

A: Yes of course, if they want to. To stop them would be to control them. People are free to believe what they want to. Obviously, if the cult is deemed as illegal then the government will be having a say.

Q: Should people be given alternative viewpoints from what their cult has indoctrinated and brainwashed them into believing?

A: Whoever is open and ready to explore, yes. Alternatives cannot be forced on anybody.

Q: Should people take responsibility for their own lives and beliefs?

A: Ideally yes, but it's important to realise that when a cult has taken over a soul, it often takes over a person's decision making with its control of that person.

Q: What can I do if my family won't have any contact with me because their cult does not allow it?

A: You are in a very difficult situation. I understand what you are going through. Ideally, can you contact others who are going through, or have been through the same challenge? During this time make sure you are in regular contact with a group and friends who will support you. Search the internet for resources and groups with ex-cult members and learn from their experiences and get advice.

Were the Exclusive Brethren that I was born into a cult?

The English Oxford Dictionary defines a cult as a system of religious veneration and devotion directed towards a particular figure or object.

When I was in the EB I had to go to eleven meetings (in the latter years ten) a week. This was the instruction of the Man of God. It was normal in every prayer in every meeting, to include prayer for our leader, who we called the Man of God, the Universal Leader, The Elect Vessel, the Leader of the Recovery of the Truth and other titles. Every month, he was sent a financial gift of a few hundred pounds just from our assembly, and I believe every single assembly around the world sent him money each month too. On every lounge wall of every house, there were prominent photos of our current leader and all previous leaders going back to J.N. Darby.

Was that a system of religious veneration and devotion directed to a particular figure?

SHAKE IT ALL ABOUT

The Man of God had tremendous power over every single member worldwide. This power controlled the type of house we were allowed to live in, the jobs we could or could not do, where we could eat, where we could sleep, who we could marry, the length of our hair, the forbidding of pets, the total ban on mobile phones, computers, TV, radio or even anything radio controlled. The power the followers gave him meant he could dictate to us what education or vocations we could not take part in, places we were not allowed to go to like cinema, theatre, sporting events or theme parks, which relatives we had to be isolated from, and the limiting of access to people, for example school friends or anyone outside the EB who obviously didn't conform to the Man of God's laws. Now, if any of the Man of God's laws were broken, that person would be cut off and shunned, and if his/her family stayed in, they would be separated or split from family members who had broken the laws.

Again, was that a system of religious veneration and devotion directed to a particular figure, or not?

If you believe it was, you will conclude that of course, the Exclusive Brethren that I was in was a cult. That's what a cult is according to the definition in the English Oxford Dictionary. I don't believe there is a judge in this world that given the above facts, could conclude anything different. Yet the EB used to maintain that they were not a cult. Why? Maybe it is because cults are associated with control, bigotry and the splitting up of families. They are not honourable attributes of any group. Cults, at least the hardcore ones, tend to leave a trail of damaged and wounded ex-members in their wake.

There are people affected by religious cults who are suffering anguish, trauma and great pain from being split from their families. This had been going on for decades. Who cares about such people? I care! Just before publishing this book I got a phone call from the EB telling me not to mention anything to do with my twenty-two years as a member? Why? Why hide the laws that we all had to go through and of which many still apply to this very day, so I'm told. What is there to hide? Instead of being offended and wanting to cover up what has gone on, why not open up dialogue, let us learn from each other, learn from mistakes, recognise and start to rectify the suffering that many are still going through. Instead of fearing questions, how about honestly scrutinising everything we believe and currently stand for? Is this asking too much?

SHAKE IT ALL ABOUT

Is the Plymouth Brethren Christian Church, the EB rebrand in 2012, still a cult?

I do not know. It depends on what their latest laws are.

CHAPTER 22

The Blind Spot.

the elephant in the room

Why did Gavrilo Princip shoot Archduke Franz Ferdinand in Sarajevo on 28th June 1914, leading to World War 1 resulting in 16 million deaths? According to his beliefs, this was the 'right' thing to do.

Why did Adolph Hitler launch an invasion of Poland on 1st September 1939, leading to World War II and 50-80 million deaths? According to his beliefs, this was the 'right' thing to do.

Why did people decide to crash planes into the World Trade Center on 9th September 2001 killing about 3000 people that day? According to their beliefs, this was the 'right' thing to do.

Why were there coordinated bombings in Madrid, on the morning of 11 March 2004, killing 193 people and injured around 2000? According to the killers' beliefs, this was the 'right' thing to do.

Why did Anders Breivik, on the 22nd July 2011, open fire on youngsters attending a summer camp on the Norwegian island of Utoya, taking 77 lives? According to his beliefs, this was the 'right' thing to do.

Why was British Army soldier, Fusilier Lee Rigby of the Royal Regiment of Fusiliers, attacked and killed by Michael Adebolajo and Michael Adebowale on 22nd May 2013? According to the killers' beliefs, this was the 'right' thing to do.

Why were 130 people killed and over 350 injured on Friday 13 November 2015 as Paris suffered a terrorist attack? According to the killers' beliefs, this was the 'right' thing to do.

On 22nd May 2017, a suicide bomber killed 22 people at an Ariana Grande concert at Manchester Arena. Why? According to his beliefs, he thought this was the 'right' thing to do.

On 3 June 2017, a terrorist vehicle-ramming and stabbing took place in London. A van was deliberately driven into pedestrians on London Bridge. Three men then ran to the nearby Borough Market area and began stabbing people in and around restaurants and pubs. Eight people were killed and 48 were injured. Why? According to their beliefs, they thought this was the 'right' thing to do.

On 15th March 2019, Brenton Tarrant killed forty-nine people and wounded 48 at two mosques in Christchurch, New Zealand, in the nation's deadliest attack. Why? According to his beliefs, he thought this was the 'right' thing to do.

All these killers had the blind spot.

Definition of a blind spot: An area where a person's view is obstructed. There is a blind spot in humanity, an obscure area that is enshrouded in mist and distraction. In fact, it is usually darkness that conceals this 'area'. It is counter-intuitive to even think about it. It is protected by fear and pride and therefore at first, is uncomfortable to even look at, hence many rather avoid it. This blind spot causes an auto-self-brainwashing effect and is the root cause of wars, murder, division, disunity, splits, schisms, separation and all-controlling cults. The blind spot is:

Believing I am 'right' about what I believe.

SHAKE IT ALL ABOUT

Ouch! But... my beliefs are right, aren't they? Consider this: anything that you believe is 'wrong,' you believe you are 'right' about it.

There are many influencing factors which cause us to have beliefs. During the times we hold a belief, we think we are 'right.' If we didn't, we wouldn't have that belief.

A person with a deep-rooted radical belief, who has been coercively controlled or brainwashed into believing, for example, one plus one equals three, no matter how you rationally prove that one plus one equals two, they will not see it. Why? A cluster of reasons have set their belief in rock hard concrete.

The main reasons are:
- Fear of the possible consequences of believing something different.
- Fear of having been wrong for maybe many decades.
- Immersing themselves only with people who believe the same thing.
- Pride and ego rising up in them to protect their 'rightness.'

Just these four traits together can cause humans to make some of the gravest of errors; killing and separating families just to name two. They bring out the traits of fear, self-righteousness, pride, separation, exclusion and condemnation of others who aren't the same as 'us.' To even begin to get free from being coercively controlled or brainwashed, requires enough humility, enough love for yourself and enough curiosity to even make you look at an alternative.

So, the blind spot is simply...
Thinking I am 'right.'

At first glance, this is not even an issue. I mean, who thinks they are wrong? Everyone has an opinion on things do they not?
Let me illustrate with a story I was once told by an old man Steve;
During school years, his mother would always leave him his dinner money on the kitchen table.
One morning he left for school and when he got there he hung his coat up in the cloakroom and went to his lessons as normal.
At dinnertime, he went to the cloakroom to get his money only to find

that it wasn't there. He remembered picking it up from the kitchen table and putting it in his pocket that morning. He was utterly convinced he had done so. He could picture himself doing it. He went and told his teacher who asked the class if anyone had taken the money. No one owned up so the teacher went to the headmaster. The headmaster assembled the whole school and since no one owned up he kept the whole school back for an hour's detention at the end of the day.

When Steve got home, he saw the money still on the kitchen table from that morning. His memory of picking it up was from the previous day. Here is then what Steve told me which has stayed with me my all my life:

"YOU CAN THINK YOU ARE SO RIGHT..... YET BE SO WRONG."

There is the blind spot. It is called self-righteousness. Have a look at the facts.

There are over 40,000 religious denominations in the world and that number is growing rapidly. Why? Because they each think they are right. The right religion, the right church, the right scriptures, the right interpretation, the right doctrines, the right rules, the right regulations and the right way of doing things.

Man generally has an aptitude which is that he has to be right. His religious denomination and his interpretation of his Holy Book isn't the third best or the tenth. It is the right one, and if it isn't quite perfect, then he knows how it should be.

King Solomon once wrote that, 'Every way of a man is right in his own eyes.' (Darby version)

If you were to put all your money on the version of your 'religion/denomination' as being the right one, the odds might be 40,000/1.

History shows that man has sought to live by his 'rightness' for millennia. A few years ago, I was shocked when I first saw that it had been my modus operandi as well. Here's what I saw;

My version of understanding of what was 'right' has always shifted, evolved and changed continually and often out of all recognition. If I am honest with myself, I have to admit that at each change, each 'latest' new understanding, I STILL CONTINUALLY BELIEVED THAT I WAS RIGHT! However, each time I amazingly forgot that my previous version was not right, and had been flawed and in error, but all I could see was that my latest version was right.

I have discovered that this is not a comfortable subject to talk about with most people. When I have had this conversation with 'very religious' people here were three of their responses.

Me: What do you say about being right about your religious beliefs, bearing in mind there are over 40,000 denominations in the world today?

Very religious person 1: "I am right."

Very religious person 2: "I just read the Bible. It is simple. Believe what it says."

Very religious person 3: "There is only one right position and speaking humbly, it is the one I am in."

Can you see? All right, according to their viewpoint. Try asking people yourself and see their response.

Where does this 'I'm right' come from?

Logically, it comes from people's differing views on how they judge the world around them according to their understanding of whether something is good or evil, right or wrong. If their knowledge is that it is good then it is judged as right. If their knowledge of it is evil, then it is judged as being wrong.

With this knowledge of good and evil, a dualism takes place. A 'them and us.' A world governed by people making judgements.

It is not difficult to see that we live in a world with vast differences in people's judgements about what is good and evil. All strife, separation, dis-ease, disease, disunity and wars, can be traced back to judgements being made and disagreed upon.

Being 'right' is what most people believe is their identity. It is what humans do. It makes sense. Hit the nail, not your thumb. Isn't it obvious?

What is the alternative? Consider this if you will.

Live by your heart and increasingly discover the amazing love inside yourself and everyone else. It's there. Explore living and moving in non-judgemental compassion rather than the old right and wrong judgement. Love everyone including yourself; unconditionally. To realise the capacity you have inside you to do this, find someone who can reveal the love inside you, someone who is perfect love and who shows you that you are too. You are made in the image and likeness of unconditional love. Don't settle for anything less.

So how about; it's not about me being 'right' anymore?

Instead, how about; Love is right.

Love, and love alone, opens up the whole vista of endless possibilities through an innocence and a child-like spirit of unconditional generosity, encouragement and fullness of life. Instead of crawling through our existence on our hands of knees with an 'I'm right, you're wrong,' belief, you are now free to soar like an eagle on the currents of love. Your intuition is now like a flowing river of living water. No more war, no more separation, no more division. Instead, everlasting love joy and peace and union for all.

In the words of Freddie, "This could be heaven for everyone."

CHAPTER 23

How To Escape The Cult You Are In
if you really want to

In this chapter, I use my personal experience from my Exclusive Brethren years, as a reference for any cult that anyone might want to get free from. Although the escape route I took will probably be different than other people's route, the principles will be the same and could, therefore, be helpful.

I know what it is like to go through the great struggle and pain that leaving a cult can cause. There was a time when I felt like I was a rope in a tug of war. My heart was being wrenched from two different directions and the best word that I use to describe what it is like is dread. I felt I was totally trapped in my situation with no way out; a place of fear and indecision. What I once was taught and totally believed, appeared to be brilliant white light and truth, but turned out to be what I now see and believe as darkness and man-made religion.

I am aware of how sensitive the subject of leaving a system of control is. I have attempted to write this chapter sensitively but forgive me if I ever appear clinical or calculating. Sometimes, tough decisions have to be made and we all have different tolerances and speeds that we are comfortable with. I take it very seriously. I am approaching this subject as if it was a matter of life or death. It is in a way. We can live our lifetime ranging from being free to live and love unconditionally, or we can be restricted and controlled by a man/woman or a system that has managed to incarcerate us in their laws and so kill the spirit in us that was meant to live free.

Here is some good news to begin with. The truth of how anyone can be set free from a cult or system of control is simple. The journey may be challenging but the principle is indeed simple. Most of the challenges are in the mind where we are threatened with the emotional stress of separation from our loved ones, fear of the unknown future, and beliefs that the situation is hopeless and too complicated. Here is that principle:

A person will leave a cult when their value to escape, is stronger than the value to stay.

Have you ever been to a Japanese water garden and watched a Shishi-Odoshi. If so, you will have watched bamboo rods fixed to a hinge, slowly filling with water until the balance shifts then whoosh, the water tips out.

In life, we only ever do what is most important to us, or that which we value the most. It is therefore 'values' that keep people in a situation that they don't want to be in. Only when you reach a tipping point in your values will you move from your current situation. This is where there is a more powerful reason to leave than to stay.

I was shocked when I first realised just how much my values are behind my decisions in my life. Values can be as important to our life as a compass is to a ship. When we identify our values and change them, if we want to, we can find the necessary motivation

and power to make needed massive life-changing decisions instead of living in paralysis. This applies not just to being trapped in a cult but any controlling situation that people find themselves in. Such is the importance of understanding this principle, I shall list eight characteristics:

SHAKE IT ALL ABOUT

1. A value is simply what is important to you.
2. Everything you hold dear to and fight to preserve stems from your own value system.
3. Values are what you stand for, what you believe in, and what you do.
4. Values make you the person you are.
5. Values provide our upfront motivation so are life or death to our potential success in anything.
6. Actions reveal your values because you always act with what is most important and valuable to you at the time.
7. People confused about their values accomplish little.
8. Conflicting values hold you back and cause stress.

Generally speaking, we only ever do what our values motivate us to do. Here are some examples of how values can direct a person's life.

Many people have a job they hate, yet the money they need to maintain their lifestyle is a greater value to them than the job they do. Therefore, they set their alarm clock to wake themselves up at 6 am every morning. Those same people who hate their job, value the security the money gives them more than even looking for another job that they love.

Some people value the feeling food gives them more than being slim. Some people value being slim more than food which causes them to be aware of what they eat.

Some people value their marriage enough to refuse to have an affair when temptation appears. Some people value spending more

time with their children than working all hours to pay for a larger house.

From every large to every small decision, our life is the manifestation of our values. Values can be the biggest motivator to any decision we make in our life. Values can also change and when they do, we change.

When I first realised that I wanted out at the age of 18, my values to stay in the EB were more powerful than my values to leave. What was most important to me was not upsetting my parents and friends and not upsetting my life of relative peace. I was trapped with too many reasons of why to stay. My values to stay controlled my life. I had to have a change of mind if I was to ever escape.

It took me four years to get to the tipping point and escape. In those four years, my values began to shift with regards to freedom from boredom and control, expressing myself, enjoying things that had been utterly forbidden like football matches, restaurants and the cinema. I didn't understand that my values had been decided for me and imprinted on my mind through repetition, tradition, culture, fear and the will of the leader of the Exclusive Brethren.

When my value for freedom from Exclusive Brethrenism became higher than my value for anything else, I changed. I escaped my situation.

This powerfully motivated me to take the necessary practical steps to leave, which were to arrange accommodation, install a phone line for my business and sort out my other needs.

I want to point out that in that moment there were still many unanswered questions that remained unanswered for years. However, I wasn't waiting until I understood everything. That's called paralysis. I was aligning to my new values and being true to myself and how I felt. In time I was to see that it was one of the greatest decisions I have made in my life.

Similarly, if your life is being controlled in any way, your values today and every day will decide what you are going to do about it. For example, what value are you putting on the familiarity of your cult life, the tradition of your peers, the 'being told what to do,' the laws that are supposed to protect you, the 'putting up and shutting up,' your 'always correct' interpretation of your Holy Book, being true to yourself, or your limited life span etc?

At this point, I want to mention what I shall call Value Perverts. These are lies that can powerfully lock false values in a person's mind often through indoctrination or brainwashing. These can burrow so deep and be so insidious that many will never ask or even consider their validity. They are usually steeped in tradition and for many are utterly unquestionable. I know this is controversial, but I invite you to just consider the following beliefs that I came to see were just lies:

If I leave my cult/religion:

- I will go to hell which will be eternal conscious torment.
- I will definitely be worse off than I am now.
- There will never be any hope for me ever.
- I will be an outcast.
- God will be angry with me and punish me.
- I will come out from under spiritual authority and will be in danger.
- I will be doing the worst thing that I could ever do.
- I will never find a full and wonderful life outside the religion I have been married to.

So far, this chapter has been majoring on one main point; Values. The aim so far has been to show that values are the pivot on which will determine whether we remain in a cultic controlled situation, or whether we will escape it.

Values Realisation Exercise – (Revealing Why You Are Where You Are)

If you are trapped in an abusive controlling situation, it is because you are trapped in your values.

Changing your values changes the priorities of your entire life. If you change your values, you change your destiny!

Sitting on the fence over a life-changing decision can be very challenging and stressful. I've mentioned already in this book how my four years of indecision felt like I was a rope in a tug of war. I was being pulled hard from both directions at the same time. It took me four years to reach my tipping point. It can take some people a lot longer.

The aim of this exercise is twofold:

1.   To help towards realising your core values which reveal the real reason why you are where you are today.

2.   To help you come to a place of a clear decision whereby you can move on with your life, one way or another.

The 21 questions enable you to deeply examine both sides of the issue. Leave the cult or stay. Your free will to choose must be respected. Cults do not respect this. However, love respects choices and does not coerce one way or another. It is your life. What do you want?

Find somewhere quiet if you can and ask yourself the following: (Best to be ruthlessly honest with yourself.)

SHAKE IT ALL ABOUT

Questionnaire:
1. What do you value most about staying?
2. What do you value most about leaving?
3. What five things might you be missing out on if you leave?
4. What five things might you be missing out on if you stay and do nothing?
5. What will it cost you to leave?
6. What will it cost you to stay?
7. What benefit would it give you by staying?
8. What benefit would it give you by leaving?
9. What will change in other areas of your life if you leave?
10. What will stay the same if you stay?
11. If you were to leave, how much would the condemnation of the cult bother you?
12. How much should you value their condemnation?
13. How much are you basing your decision to stay on how others think or feel about you?
14. How much do you value making the most of the remaining years that you have left in your life?
15. How important to you is obeying a system that intends to keep you under its control through its laws and rules?
16. How much do you value the adventure of going into the unknown, the excitement of exploring life free from cultic law you have been under?
17. How do you feel about staying where you are so that you can continue the same relationship with family and friends?
18. How does leaving, and by your example, family and friends might also leave in time, sound to you?
19. What 3 reasons are most important to you that would make you want to stay where you are? What else?
20. What 3 reasons are most important to you that would make you want to leave where you are? What else?

These questions lead to this one final question:

21. What one reason of highest value to you, would tip you into making a total commitment to yourself, right now, one way or the other?

SHAKE IT ALL ABOUT

By asking yourself these 21 questions, you will have been feeling and realising your values, those things that are important to you. They have been the motivations in your life so far. Most people have values that motivate them to leave whilst at the same time have values that motivate them to remain where they are. This is a conflict of values and they can block a person from moving forward freely.

In the four years that I was struggling about wanting to leave, the conflict of values caused me the unhappiness that comes from indecision or double-mindedness. The pain of this unhappiness eventually exploded on my 22nd birthday when my mind became awakened to two brand new values. (1) The fear that in 10 years' time I would have been 32, and if I did not take (2) personal responsibility immediately, I would be guaranteed to be starting another 10 years of unhappiness/misery.

The fear of this reality of 10 more years, coupled with the awareness that only I could take responsibility to prevent this, gave me the clarity I needed. It was as if the sun came out and dispersed the fog of indecision and procrastination. Now I knew what I really wanted or more to the point, what I didn't want. My new values now empowered me to act single-mindedly.

However, it's important to note that despite making the clear commitment to leave, I still had a conflict of values going on, but these were now not powerful enough to override my top two values. If I had waited for all my values to align, I'd still be trapped today. I left exhilarated by my honouring of my top two values yet saddened by the conflicting values that I still had. For those, healing and the coming to terms with those conflicts needed to take place. They took place over time!

The following lists show my top 10 values before and after my overriding decision to leave. (Because they were personal to me, they might not make sense to everyone).

My top ten values and conflicts before I escaped.
Pleasing my parents
Family values
Keeping the peace
Friendships
Freedom/Liberation (A conflict of values)

Prosperity (A conflict of values)
Excitement (A conflict of values)
People-pleasing (A conflict of values)
Curiosity (A conflict of values)
Secrecy (A conflict of values)

My top ten values and conflicts when I escaped.
Fear (Of 10 more years of unhappiness)
Responsibility (My life is down to me)
Pleasing my parents (Still a massive conflict of values)
Excitement
Self-respect
Freedom/Liberation
Curiosity
Family values (Still a conflict of values)
People-pleasing (Still a conflict of values)
Friendships (Still a conflict of values)

If you feel it would help you, make two lists. One with your top 10 values at the moment. Then next to it, a list that would include values that would give you the motivation to make the decision to leave. Remember the question before, "What one reason of highest value to you, would tip you into making a commitment to yourself, right now, one way or the other?" To leave your situation, your values will have to be greater than what they are to you staying in your situation. Can you see what new values you would need or what values you would have to change to cause you to make that life-changing decision to leave?

This exercise is not a science, but it can be a massive help in understanding ourselves and our motivations. In an ideal situation, a person could change all 10 values with no conflicts. This would give them every reason to leave their situation with the minimum of difficulty. For those who have what I had, still a conflict in some of their values, it makes leaving still a potentially difficult challenge.

However, to get to a tipping point and actually make that decision to leave, your revised / new values HAVE TO BE MORE IMPORTANT TO YOU than the previous ones.

As Tony Robbins states, "You can't always control the wind, but you can control your sails".

My new values were powerful enough to overcome the pain of leaving my parents and all the people I knew, including the indoctrination and 'pleasing God' under the EB laws.

We end up doing what we value the most. I recommend you taking time to really evaluate your values, and if you can do so, with the help of friends, family and faith to help elicit the values.

If you are unhappy yet not sure that you should break free and escape your situation, I suggest it is simply that your value of staying is at the moment greater than your value of being free from your past and your present.

Consider this reality check:

In ten years' time, you will be ten years older and maybe ten years longer in a controlled, smothering, disrespecting-your-free-will environment. Yes, the people may be sincere but how about you being sincere with yourself? I came to the place of valuing my free will higher, than submitting to those who insisted they control and abuse it. In other words, if you realise you are unhappy failing to keep other's rules and laws, then be honest with yourself. Go! You might just find as I did, that God isn't a law wielding, rule demanding, regulation changing, strict disciplinarian that many poor controlled souls are being coercively indoctrinated into yielding to right now. You might even find that God actually loves everyone unconditionally! Imagine that! Being true to the new values that I realised, and looking back now, I can clearly see that it was one of the best things I have done in my life. Phew!

If on the other hand, you feel at this time that your values in staying are more powerful than your values to leave, then why not commit yourself to staying? Sometimes it is about choosing the right time, the right time for you. Maybe if you leave, your family will stay and there would be a family split. Accept your situation, at least for now. You can always revisit this values exercise in the future. Keep on searching and you will find. Where there is a will there is a way.

Lastly, if you have come to that place of a decision to leave, don't do it alone. You are not alone. There are many resources that can really help you and where you will be able to talk to people. Have a look at the Help page at the website below and take courage, there's more to life than being controlled, it's called freedom.

www.cult-escape.com

CHAPTER 24

Religious Transparency

a legislation proposal

Imagine a son or daughter is suddenly separated from their father and mother. What was once a happy family living together, sharing life with each other, there for each other, who had always celebrated special occasions and all the important events in life together, comes to an abrupt end. The family is now separated. This separation could last for months, years or even for life.

As the reality of this terror sinks in, that son or daughter feels like a dagger has severed their heart in two. Instead of familiar smiles and hugs from their parents and siblings, an icy shield has now come down. There is now an emotional disconnect, a feeling of loss and the heavy heart that a bereavement brings. What was once happiness and acceptance has suddenly turned to suspicion, awkwardness and condemnation. They are being judged as evil, they have been cut off from their family and are now shunned. No more eating together, no more living in the same house, no more holidays, birthdays or wedding invites. Something has had a powerful influence over that once happy family.

What is that powerful influence?

SHAKE IT ALL ABOUT

These separations cause great suffering. When an infant is separated from its mother, for whatever reason, as the awful reality sinks in that the relationship is no longer there, that child can experience great anguish. That child may scream with the pain and the loss of its mother. Well, adults that are cut off from their loved ones feel that pain too, but often, they just suffer in silence.

I was one of those people.

I have often wondered…. Should there not be governmental protection?

May I ask you a question?

What should we do when something is socially unacceptable, yet it is legal? I did a survey on LinkedIn to find out the public perception of cultic separation. The question was:

In your view, how acceptable and 'right' is it for families to be separated by 'cult law?'

The following are all the comments by people that answered the question. All were asked if they wanted their name or initials included. Some wanted to remain anonymous:

1: Family are the MOST important support network you can have. Unless your entire family are abusers, cutting all contact seems to me, abusive and constitute "cruel and unusual" treatment. I don't know how I would have coped without siblings and parents/grandparents. Anon

2: I struggle to imagine enforced separation and my imagination certainly doesn't stretch to anyone believing it could ever be a good idea (except where literal danger is present). FB

3: How acceptable? Completely and entirely Unacceptable. Any "religion" that seeks to divide, control and manipulate its members and followers is a cult based on its own power and not the higher power or love of any god or the greater good. D Walker

4: Separation of families like many other cultic behaviours is a mechanism of control. Jill Mytton.

5: It's not as it impinges basic freedoms. Religion and faith are supposed to embrace love, aren't they? Sarah Jones

6: It's all about control, power and money. They will do anything to obtain this absolutely anything even if it means separating families. Because if you have unity with family this gives you power and they fear this. It's very wrong and all cults like this should face some type of criminal punishment. Sharon Byrne

7: The Jehovah's Witnesses cult that I was raised in proclaims 'God is Love' but turns their members against those 'Apostates' that reject the JW teachings. Brian Hunt

8: I'd agree with separation of families (or anyone) for protection from abuse, negative influence etc. In my view, it's just cruel to impose this within a cult setting and maybe should be illegal like in other areas of life where deprivation of liberty is not acceptable. Kris M

9: It is not 'right'! End of. This subject makes me very unhappy. To have your true emotional needs replaced by counterfeit ones imposed by others is toxic. This is the way the leaders of cults can control others. Anon

10: I don't find that acceptable. Hearts must break constantly. I've watched a documentary on this and it's just so difficult to watch. Cults to me are control and power. Nichola Robinson

11: I watched Leah Remini's documentary on it, truly frightening how easy it is to con people with a vision..........when you take a weak person and strip them back to nothing. Mike Wagstaff

12: Can't think of anything worse John. Family is everything and the rest of work enablers to be with family. Mike Holmes

13: It's just so cruel John, I can't imagine what kind of monsters would do this to children. Jeanne Hatton

14: It's wrong, John. This is where authorities should intervene because separating children from family members without good reason (e.g. if they've subjected them to assault or failed to protect them from harm such as by allowing a violent person to live with them) amounts to emotional abuse. Those children grow up to be adults who have been conditioned to think they can't make their own choices and the cycle continues. Kate

15: I have friends who were in religious groups and they got out. It's so sad to hear them talk about their parents, children and grandchildren that they are barred from seeing. So sad. Gail Page

16: It's wrong, wrong, wrong. We know that people need people so anything that advocates isolation and reliance on only a small, segregated community should immediately set alarm bells ringing. This should be the first part of any training that we do for children on keeping safe. Don't keep secrets, be a part of as many groups and communities as possible and be very wary of anyone who tells you that is a bad thing. Anyone who cares for your wellbeing would want you to be engaged with others and included in their lives, not isolated. Helen

Hart

17: It makes my blood boil John. I believe people should be able to do what they want, as long as it does not impact on others. This behaviour is the total antithesis of my interpretation of humanity, enacted by ego-driven megalomaniacs. Chris Gilsenan

18: Not acceptable at all ... I'm sure the God or Gods these religions look up to were as evil as these laws they wouldn't be getting looked up to at all. When humans have power it does strange things to some. Mick Ryan

19: These so-called "rules" are not designed to consider the emotional needs or rights of members. They are abusive control strategies with far-reaching psychological implications. Anon

20: I find your story fascinating and can't imagine what life would be like being separated from family members. Paul Corcoran

21: TOTALLY UNACCEPTABLE. Gosh John - I didn't know THAT bit. Where the hell do these cults get their wacky and damaging ideas from? Pam Case.

22: The belief in strength in a united family is, I would have thought, is a globally acceptable norm...save for the cults and other anomalies. Ches Moulton

23: That's astonishing John - and utterly unacceptable. Anon

24: It's taking away peoples right for a choice......you can only have one or the other and not both. As a parent I don't understand what could be stronger and more important than the want to be with your child?? Christina Smith

25: Personally, I would have nothing to do with such 'cult' or 'religion' that separates human, let alone families. Ashualec

26: This is such a huge subject. In my personal life, I lost my mother and her new family when they entered a religious sect and in my professional life, I mostly encounter the adult children of JW family groups, who have been ostracised and cut off from all the social and peer groups they grew up with. Steve Cordingley

27: Social services do their best not to do this when removing children from dangerous familial situations.....presumably for good reason. My friend adopted a son and they still maintain contact with his siblings through the foster family. And they've been encouraged to do so. So if this is the case in these situations I can't accept that cult law should be allowed to usurp the right to retain familial relationships where safe to do so. Jo S

28: It is so sad to cut people off because they think or want to do things differently. Kaye

29: I can't imagine being separated from mine. I don't imagine most people would even know this happens to be honest. Lorna

30: Cult laws don't supersede the law of the land. They don't have the right to separate families because some 'guru' says so. It's manipulation and mind control. Clayton Jones

31: John, religions of all types invent their own man-made rules to maintain power and control over their members, and others. Any rules that cause pain and suffering should be condemned as inhuman. John Legg

32: I very strongly disagree with the separation due to cult 'laws'/ restrictions. Anon

Whilst the sample size is small, I don't think it is unreasonable to conclude that most people generally find cultic separation totally unacceptable.

Is this how you feel about it?

Cultic law can influence families to separate from members who disobey them. These cultic laws are not implemented and enforced by the governments of where these people live. They are imposed by religious cults that have indoctrinated their followers and have got into their heads. Such is the power that some cults can have over their followers, parents and children will abandon each other, husbands and wives will leave each other, and families will separate. This power over people has even led some groups to commit mass suicide. I say this not to be dramatic but because it has actually happened in the past. Could it happen in the future?

But can anyone start a religious cult and start imposing their own laws on vulnerable followers?

Yes.

The right to do this is supported by The Human Rights Act 1998 in which are the following two Articles:

Article 9: Freedom of thought, conscience and religion. Everyone is free to hold a broad range of views, beliefs and thoughts, and to follow a religious faith. The right to manifest those beliefs may be limited only in specified circumstances.

Article 10: Freedom of expression. Everyone has the right to hold opinions and express their views on their own or in a group. This applies even if these views are unpopular or disturbing. This right can be restricted only in specified circumstances.

If you read these two articles in full, you will notice that the words 'protection and rights' are used many times.

Because of the freedoms in the Human Rights Act, it is not illegal for anyone to start a religious cult and effectively control their followers to give them their money, adopt their peculiar belief system, die rather than take blood and if the rest of their follower's family do not also obey, then they may find that they end up ostracising and split from them. This can result in a family destroyed by separation.

I am not suggesting that government bans religious organisations that split families. People have the freedom to join whatever group they want to. However, where is the protection for vulnerable people who are born into, or are recruited into religious groups which results in their vulnerable family being split? Specifically, what are their rights?

Is there something that can be done......?

Governments have the difficult job of striking a balance between being too restrictive which can infringe on freedoms and being too liberal, which can also infringe on freedoms.

The purpose of government is to protect the individual rights of its citizens. This covers most departments of our life including Health and Safety. When a government deems something to be a potential danger it issues what are known as Government Health Warnings. Such warnings are not always bans but they are put in place to educate and protect. This is what responsible government does and it is what we expect and vote for them to do.

Precedents.

1.   'Prevent' is part of the Government's counter-terrorism strategy. It draws attention to ideology that supports terrorism with a view to protecting vulnerable people. It highlights sectors and institutions where there are risks of radicalisation.

2.   Government believe it necessary to enforce the publishing of health warnings on cigarette packets. They have not banned tobacco, but maybe it was enough destroyed lives that eventually motivated them to legislate a warning to all who smoke, or who might be thinking of smoking.

3.   The PPI scandal in principle was that people were not informed about what they were paying for. When what was happening came to

light, banks were told to pay back what was due resulting in millions seeking compensation. To prevent this from happening in the future, the Financial Services Authorities brought in a new regime in 2011 which included customers having to be told in writing that PPI was an optional extra.

I think it is imperative that there is consideration for new legislation in the UK that seeks to a) promote awareness and b) to be a warning to all people about religious cults who have laws in place, that result in the SEPARATION of FAMILIES. Specifically, I'm referring to the separation that results in cult members not being allowed to have 'normal family life' with non-members. (definition below).

My definition of 'normal family life'.

1. Families are allowed and free to live together if desired.
2. Families are allowed and free to visit each other in their homes and stay with each other.
3. Families are allowed to freely celebrate the birth of their grandchildren and family weddings.
4. Families are allowed to fully join in freely with the funeral arrangements of family members.
5. Families are allowed to freely celebrate birthdays and special occasions.
6. Families are allowed to eat or drink freely with each other anywhere.
7. Families are allowed to freely go out shopping together.
8. Families are allowed to freely go on holidays together.

With this in mind, I would like society and the government to consider the following:

I would like to see religious groups that impose laws, whereby members/followers cannot have or are unable to maintain this 'normal family life', having some form of religious transparency warning on all literature and as a readable sign on any buildings where they meet.

I would also like to recommend that the first time anyone comes into contact with such a group, they must be read this warning in full and sign a document indicating that they have understood it. I would also like to see this applying to all existing members.

The Goal of the religious transparency warning:

1: The public will be better placed to able to make informed decisions, should they choose to join such religious groups that separate families, resulting in there being a protective measure in place for this socially unacceptable destruction of normal family life.

CHAPTER 25

My Conclusion

What could be the most effective solution to ending the abuse, harm and damage that thousands of religious cults are inflicting on their followers today? As outrageous as it may sound, I believe the most effective solution is something we can all activate right now, if we choose to.

I shall put my neck on the line further by saying that the reason it took 28 years to start to write this book, was that I had been waiting for this solution. Read on.

Actually, 'solution' is not the best word to use. Nowadays we are used to instant solutions, quick fixes and logical answers that make perfect sense. What I am going to try and describe is not necessarily short term or long term. It is something almost timeless and might be better grasped with intuition rather than logical analysis. I'll attempt to illustrate it. Here goes.

Law Enforcement or Unconditional Love?

Law Enforcement, such as rules and regulations do not work, inasmuch as they do not generally produce inner change. Religious law forces people to conform through fear instead of allowing effective transformation. It is the method that cultic religions employ to control their members or followers. The leader or system decides the laws that must be obeyed. They update their laws at will. The laws are enforced

SHAKE IT ALL ABOUT

with the spoken or unspoken threat of punishment should a law be broken. This does not stop their laws being broken but it is the only way they know to try to control their members. In essence, this control always has its root in fear. The power of control over their subjects is determined by their level of coercive control, brainwashing and the severity of the punishment that follows any disobedience.

For example, you might be a woman who wears jeans and who has cut your hair. Or you may be a man who has a moustache and a car radio. Imagine if getting caught having these things could result in you never seeing your husband, wife or children ever again? How ridiculous you might be thinking! I am not living in fear of being punished for having those things you might say. No, that is because you are not under the control of the cults that have such laws. If you were, and there are many people today who have been punished this way, you would be under this type of law enforcement.

For those committed and immersed in a cult, they don't feel law is being enforced. They willingly submit to the 'truth' of their leader. Following his 'truth' is attractive to them because they want to please their leader and it makes them feel like they are on the right path. However, step over that line and the leader and the whole group will ostracise them in a moment. Without realising it, the followers are under cultic law enforcement.

So, to use the same principle of law enforcement against such cults would be playing them at their own game. You could fight them, threaten them and punish them in whatever way you could. It would be 'eye for an eye, tooth for a tooth retaliation.' That's reasonable some would say, but it would just be law enforcement that doesn't work and therefore ultimately fails.

A more excellent way; Unconditional Love.

What would happen if everyone loved each other unconditionally?

Would there be wars, fighting, strife, violence, separation, division, hatred, jealousy, unforgiveness, bitterness, resentment, greed, theft, fear, rape, slavery, abuse, racism, prejudice, cultic control and anything else you can think of which people get hurt by?

Well, no, but not everyone does love each other unconditionally, at the moment, so what's the relevance John?

I remember as a child, hearing an old quote from JN Darby's father. JN

SHAKE IT ALL ABOUT

Darby was one of the first prominent leaders of the Brethren movement, back in the early 1830s. His father told him, "Make it better by one."

Therefore, my conclusion is simply this:

My dear Brothers and Sisters, members of the Exclusive Brethren from my past, some now called members of the Plymouth Brethren Christian Church today, and including every man who has been called the Man of God:

I love you all unconditionally. I totally forgive you for influencing my family to follow your laws, that resulted in my precious family being split up from my four grandparents, uncles, aunts, cousins, then later influencing my loving parents, and all the friends that I grew up with, whereby they have shunned me for the last 30 years.

I have no demands on you. I accept you as you are, and my hope is that you receive my love and that you are blessed in growing in the knowledge of the eternal, never failing, unconditional, uniting love of God.

I bless you all.

Love John.

Was there another purpose to going through this experience of cultic control and family separation?

Maybe so, introduced with this next question. If believing and knowing you are perfectly loved is what brings about the end to war, division and hatred, and the beginnings of peace, unity and goodwill to all, how can a person get to that place of knowing this for themselves?

As an illustration; how can you really know what an orange tastes like unless you are given one to taste? How can you get to know what any person really looks like unless you get to see them? How can you really recognise a piece of music unless you have heard it? How can you really feel unconditionally loved unless you have experienced it personally?

Surely, to know that you are loved you have to experience it personally. It's no use just reading about it or studying it. Love is not a concept or a theory. It is a living experience that you have to be open to receive, for it to be effective for you. There is lots of love in this world. Unfortunately, most of it is conditional love; you will be loved and accepted if you keep me happy, obey my rules, eat your sprouts, do your homework, earn enough money, wash regularly, don't do anything to upset me and a million other conditions. Is that really love?

Has the love you have received healed you? Has it dissolved the fear and trauma of the past and enabled you to live and love each day with peace in your heart? The love that healed me from the wounds of a shattered family was unconditional love. What is unconditional love? Here are eight ways that go towards defining what it is like to be unconditionally loved:

- You are totally accepted just as you are with no demands or qualifications.
- You are loved forever without any conditions whatsoever.
- You are loved forever no matter what condition you are in.
- You are cared for without any thought for what the carer might get for themselves.
- You are loved with an everlasting love.
- You are always freely loved even if you were ever unlovable.
- You are forgiven freely with no demand or requirement to pay anything back.
- You are loved so much that someone would die for you even if you were their enemy.

Where can this unconditional love be found? Consider the following questions:

What place accepts you unconditionally just as you are?
What is there in this world that has no demands on you?
What institution accepts you without the need for any qualifications?
What religion puts zero requirements on you?
What organisation has no expectations on you whatsoever?
Who has actually died for you personally even while you were rejecting them, proving their love is unconditional?
Where can you find total acceptance and forgiveness with no payment necessary?

Who says they love you with eternal unconditional love?

In my 53 years on Earth, as I write this, I have only ever found one reference that totally fulfils this standard of unconditional love. I don't know about you but without knowing I am loved freely this way, I cannot go on. I cannot meet the demands of any of religion's laws, rules, regulations, expectations, burdens, divisions, denominations, separations, and you know what; I am not going to continue trying. I've given up on man's religion. I've been there, done that. If I can't be accepted for being me then sorry, I have failed.

However, I am not going to end this book and conclusion without letting out a secret, an astounding discovery actually. Yes, I might be sticking my neck out and get misunderstood as preaching, but if so, that's not my intention and I'm sorry if it offends you. Here goes:
I don't believe God is 'religious.'
I believe God is Love, unconditional Love, and His Son, Jesus Christ is probably the most misunderstood man that ever lived. Man wielding religion killed his body.
I found that he actually loves me unconditionally, and not just me, but he loves everyone too.
Even when I rejected him, wasn't interested in him, was deceived into being scared of him, he died for me. This revealed that even at my worst, I was totally forgiven, accepted and loved forever. When I believed this, peace came, and the process of realising my healing had started. I believed that he is alive and offering his unconditional love to everyone freely. To receive it, there's absolutely nothing that we have to do except believe. We are what we believe. I realised that there is no other name you can believe on that offers you the unconditional love needed to free you from the wounds, baggage, scars, mistakes, guilt, men's religions and burdens of our entire life. When I believed in Jesus and his love for me, I became awakened to the love in me too, and the love in everyone. My life is now about growing in the knowledge and awareness of what it means to be loved unconditionally.

After the religious cultic experiences I was born into and lived through, I really want to say this. To believe in Jesus and know his unconditional love for you, you are not required to become a 'religious,' church going, bible bashing, goody-two-shoes Christian who has the monopoly on 'being right' and makes no mistakes. This Jesus I have spoken about, who loves me and us all unconditionally, is not the Jesus of man's religion that is riddled with traditions, conditions, divisions, laws and rules. We can access him freely by faith alone, now. All are included.

SHAKE IT ALL ABOUT

I am not suggesting you conform to a religion, rather I point you to receiving Unconditional Love.

I finish this chapter and this book with ten quotes that have helped me. My prayer and desire for you is that the great deception of man's religion, all of them, with their laws and stipulations and conditions, would not entice you away from the unconditional Love that is waiting for you right now.

- "Great happiness of life is the conviction that we are loved." Victor Hugo.
- "Love never fails." Paul the Apostle.
- "All you need is Love." Lennon/McCartney.
- "Love conquers all things; let us too surrender to love." Virgil.
- "There is no fear in love; but perfect love casts out all fear. We love because he first loved us." John the Beloved.
- "In dreams and in love, there are no impossibilities." János Arnay.
- "I love you, and that's the beginning and end of everything." F. Scott Fitzgerald.
- "He is more myself than I am. Whatever our souls are made of, his and mine are the same." Emily Bronte.
- "God is Love. Whoever lives in love lives in God, and God in them." John the Beloved.
- "This is how we know what love is. That Jesus Christ laid down his life for us." John the Beloved.

Only believe.

ABOUT THE AUTHOR

Once upon a time, to be precise, two days before Bobby Moore lifted the World Cup in 1966, a baby boy was born in Liverpool, England. He weighed in at 8lb 8oz, was the second of four boys and his delighted parents were Raymond and Eunice Spinks. They called him John.

His Dad had been born in Childwall, Liverpool, and his Mum, Croydon in Surrey England. Both were born into a Christian sect that was called the Exclusive Brethren. There were about 45,000 members, mostly in Australia, the UK and America.

His Dad started work at the Midland bank in Castle Street, Liverpool. His Mum was a secondary school general science teacher at a boy's school in Croydon. She came up to Liverpool to see friends, met his Dad, they married and were still happily married more than 50 years later.

So, John's parents started to bring up their 4 boys according to their religious beliefs. The particular schism of 'Plymouth Brethren' their parents were members of, was led by one man with a main title; 'The Man of God'. Eleven meetings a week and many laws, rules and regulations all kept the family conformed to the compulsory lifestyle as enforced by this man. The dire consequences for disobedience kept their minds focused on his 'truth'.

Growing up, John and his family's secret-from-the-world lifestyle, seemed as normal to them as brushing your teeth twice a day. However, in time, a conflict of values developed and his older brother Andrew left home at the age of 16. John left when he was 22 and his next brother Peter, left when he was 26. Their youngest brother Stephen stayed and got married and is still there to this day. The brothers knew that once they left the Exclusive Brethren, their family and friends would be separated from them by their Man of God's laws that they were under, and therefore would not be allowed to have anything to do with them.

The years of separation went by, life continued, their family divided. Then one morning in 2017, John was to wake up with an overwhelming feeling of compassion for those who know they are trapped in a cultic religion yet can't get out. He remembered his own years of struggle and torment and the feeling like he was a rope in a tug of war. He felt compelled to tell his story of what had happened in those years while in the Exclusive Brethren. He knew that many people all over the world, stuck in religious cults like he had been, needed hope, encouragement and a way out from being controlled. Freedom was and is available. Maybe just maybe, his story could help someone. Cult Escape was born.

Hello, I'm John, it's nice to meet you.

Now I know the Cult Escape title might sound a little dramatic. However, I reckon it describes what was required for me, to escape that is, and for many who are still today incarcerated by controlling religion.

Maybe, my greatest qualification for this book is just the love and passion I feel for those trapped. I also reckon I have not been ready to write this book until now. My character was too wounded and it would have blunted the message. Though I don't hold back in exposing the traditions of man that separate families and destroy so many lives, I aim for unconditional love to all people no matter who they are. Unconditional love will dissolve all separation and war and without believing that, this book would have just been a criticism without a solution.

Other interests in life led me to gain a Master Life Coaching certificate and Diploma in Psychology. I also got a first degree in Media Studies majoring in photography which is still a passion of mine. I am a Restorative Justice Counsellor and a Relationship Coach with an ambitious course I created called The Answer – Literal Steps to Your Relationship Bliss.

I am a father of an amazing daughter and I live on the Wirral Peninsular in England. I describe myself as non-religious as I love God who I believe is also non-religious. I see love and religion as opposites. My belief nowadays is that God is right, and he loves me and you unconditionally.

In writing the book, I decided to go 'raw-revealing' and say what life literally was like, trying to live under the laws of the Exclusive Brethren. I am past caring about reputation and I am not shy. Also, to date, for the last 30 years, half my family have been forbidden to sit down and have a meal with me. They are still under their old Exclusive Brethren doctrine of separation. I reached acceptance and peace about all that years ago, but the deep passion I feel, has motivated me to write it all down. I want to tell you about what it was like growing up being coercively indoctrinated with 11 meetings a week. I reveal how what I believe was spiritual abuse and control, and how it was interwoven in many areas of my life, and how my mind was groomed to be a clone of the Leader's choosing.

I will tell you my escape route in detail and how the psychological and emotional chains were far harder to break than the physical ones. What I'd like my story to achieve is to give the message that freedom from any controlling religion, is possible. Though the escape route may be different from mine, the many principles that I applied, will be relevant no matter what religion a person might be in. I really believe that there is hope for everyone.

But there's more. A person can leave a cult but does the cult ever leave the person? After escaping I spent a wild two years exploring my desires. I was driven by wounds of rejection and not feeling loved. I tell of my adventures and vices and mistakes in the book. I want to show that a person leaving a cult can make many mistakes but don't let that stop you. My journey of healing and wholeness had just begun and looking back all I needed was faith, hope and above all, love. I really believe that there is hope for 'the cult to leave a person' too.

I'm with you on your journey.

Love John

Read more and get in touch at: www.cult-escape.com

Made in United States
North Haven, CT
22 October 2023

43068436R10115